WILFRIED SONNENTHAL'S
Memories of the
WAFFEN-SS

Wilfried Sonnenthal *with* Rolf Michaelis

WILFRIED SONNENTHAL'S *Memories of the* WAFFEN-SS

An SS Radioman with the SS-Karstwehr-Bataillon Remembers

Schiffer Publishing Ltd

4880 Lower Valley Road • Atglen, PA 19310

Other Schiffer Books by the Author:
Cavalry Divisions of the Waffen-SS (978-0-7643-3661-4)
The Kaminski Brigade (978-0-7643-3765-9)
Panzer Divisions of the Waffen-SS (978-0-7643-4477-0)

Other Schiffer Books on Related Subjects:
The Cruel Hunters: SS-Sonderkommando Dirlewanger by French L. MacLean (978-0-7643-0483-5)
Police Battalions of the Third Reich by Stephen Campbell (978-0-7643-2771-1)
Commanders of Auschwitz by Jeremy Dixon (978-0-7643-2175-7)

Originally published as *SS Funker mit Bandenkampfabzeichen*,
© 2016 by Rolf Michaelis, Berlin, Germany.
Translated from the German by David Johnston

Library of Congress Control Number: 2017951875

Type set in Trade Gothic and Minion
ISBN: 978-0-7643-5464-9
Printed in China

Published by Schiffer Publishing, Ltd.
4880 Lower Valley Road
Atglen, PA 19310
Phone: (610) 593-1777; Fax: (610) 593-2002
E-mail: Info@schifferbooks.com
Web: www.schifferbooks.com

Contents

Preface 6
Chapter 1: My Youth and Entry into the *Waffen-SS* 7
Chapter 2: With the *SS-Karstwehr-Bataillon* 15
Chapter 3: The End of the War and After 41

Appendices
Appendix 1: The History of the
24. Waffen-Gebirgs[Karstjäger]-Division der SS 50
Appendix 2: The Anti-Partisan War Badge 84

Preface

In 1991, I began researching the *SS-Karstwehr-Bataillon* in preparation for a new book. At that time there were no books or other information about this unknown unit. I made contact with a number of ex-members of this small SS formation and while the former SS leaders (officers) of the battalion and later *Waffen-Gebirgs[Karstjäger]-Brigade der SS* had no interest in a book about their wartime actions in the Italian–Slovenian theater of war, the survivors from the other ranks were very taken with the idea. One of them was Wilfried Sonnenthal, who—despite suffering from Parkinson's disease—assisted me for many years until his death in 2001, devoting much time and personal effort to my work.

Not only did he describe his wartime experiences, he also made available personal documents and photographs, and I have therefore decided to turn these into a book. Wilfried Sonnenthal was a helpful, humorous man who took particular joy in music (singing) and in nature—in particular ornithology. During his service as a radio operator in the *Karstwehr-Bataillon* he experienced the disarming of the Italian Army in 1943, the actions against the Tito partisans in 1944, the expansion of the battalion into a nominal division, and in 1945 the retreat to Germany as a member of the headquarters company.

His memories include much information about the war against the partisans in Italy and the Operations Zone Adriatic Coastland, to which I have added chapters on the history of the *SS-Karstjäger* and the creation of the Anti-Partisan Badge.

Rolf Michaelis
Berlin, July 2016

Chapter 1
My Youth and Entry into the *Waffen-SS*

I was born in Württemberg on February 17, 1925, and in the summer of 1931, at the age of six and a half, I began attending the *Volksschule*. I left it seven years later in 1938, as a thirteen-year-old boy and in 1939, at the age of fourteen I began an apprenticeship to become a wholesale salesman. The training lasted three years, and at the age of seventeen years and two months I was a commercial clerk. They say that children today are generally more mature than before … but there is no one today who has his clerk's assistant letter patent at the age of seventeen.

Like almost everyone in my generation I was a member of the Hitler Youth (HJ). I enjoyed the service and I gave so much of myself that I even became a Hitler Youth leader. I can only speak for myself, but for me it was a good time. We helped farmers bring in the harvest, made crafts for various occasions, took part in fundraising campaigns with collection boxes for deserving causes or collected scrap such as paper, glass, or metal for recycling. One could also earn a few pennies at this and when work was done purchase sour candy or something sweet.

My father Willy Sonnenthal was, like many in our region, very religious. But despite his Christian beliefs, after the seizure of power he joined the German Labor Front (DAF) as a master painter. The beginning economic upturn as well as a certain pressure from the party and the DAF had led to this. My dear father was not very happy—neither about <u>his</u> membership in the DAF nor <u>mine</u> in the Hitler Youth. Unfortunately, I had little time for his ideas, and he was too liberal and good-natured to turn against his son. I was already too much under the spell of National-Socialism, but he regretted his "submission" to National-Socialism and in the summer of 1938, just after I had finished at the *Volksschule*, he abruptly dropped out of the DAF. He explained this by stating that he was guided only by what was in the Bible. Of course the Party was dismayed to hear this and there were inevitable consequences.

The NSDAP's "charming" *Kreisleiter* in Heilbronn, Richard Drauz,* was so furious about it that he officially directed the Heilbronn Chamber of Crafts and the District Master Craftsman of Heilbronn not to offer or give my father any more contracts. Thus the face of National-Socialism showed one of its facets: "If you are not one of us, we have many ways of making your life difficult." Drauz's agitation didn't have much effect, though, for my father had never received any public projects anyway. And, as a rule, private customers didn't care much for the *Kreisleiter*, mainly because of the verbal outbursts for which he was known. I even believe that many from our town took off their hats to my father in spirit and afterward had more respect for him than had been the case before. As said, at that time piousness was widespread in the countryside in Württemberg, and a devout Catholic "had" to be at odds with National-Socialism. At the time I was of the opinion that my father had not behaved very intelligently, because he could have remained in the DAF without much effort. But he had his line and I am very proud that he did not become a follower, as I had done rather uncritically. He died in 1992.

I worked as a commercial employee from April to October 1942, and on October 6 that year I was called up to do my Reich Labor service. I was promoted to foreman after just four weeks, which was rather unusual. Until December 28, 1942, I belonged to RAD Battalion 4/271 in Renchen. One day a *Waffen-SS* recruiting team showed up there, spoke pithily and urged us to join the wonderful *Waffen-SS*. "It is expected, of course, that Hitler Youth leaders will volunteer!" Barely eighteen years of age, even I found their agitation rather boyish. One actually couldn't describe it as a pure "recruiting campaign." Instead we were all more or less overpowered and I believe that some parents later complained. We were given no opportunity to reflect, and that same lunchtime we were required to give our signature. I know that several refused to sign. The response of the *Waffen-SS* recruiters was to immediately become coarse, derogatory, and offensive: "If you still want to play with dolls, then just go home to your mummy."

I spent Christmas and New Year's in a homey atmosphere with my parents. My spirits were perhaps a little depressed by the changes at the front in Germany's disfavor. I had a map of Europe hanging on the wall of my room and I always marked the position of the front, as reported in the *Wehrmacht* communiqués, the newspapers,

*Richard Drauz was born in Heilbronn on April 2, 1894 and in 1932 he became *Kreisleiter* in Heilbronn. Because of his numerous leading and managing posts in various companies, associations, and unions, he had considerable influence on the social and economic issues of his district. Taking advantage of these positions, he approached companies—for example the food maker Knorr—and denounced them if they did not respond favorably to his wish to exert influence at the management level. His coarse character made him unpopular. Even within the NSDAP he was tried several times in the internal NSDAP district court. Toward the end of the Second World War, Drauz showed an even worse side of his character. On April 3, 1945, he had the deputy *Ortsgruppenleiter* of Heilbronn-Sontheim summarily executed, because he had not prevented an anti-tank barricade from being removed. Drauz had a cardboard sign hung from the body bearing the words "*I am a traitor to the people*". When he left Heilbronn three days later and saw white flags hanging from the windows of several houses, he ordered the inhabitants immediately shot. Drauz subsequently found shelter under a false name in the Dernbach Monastery near Montabaur, but in July 1945, he was arrested by the CIC. The Americans had been looking for him for his part in the shooting of an American pilot on March 24, 1945. On December 11, 1945 an American military court in Dachau sentenced him to death as a war criminal. One year later, on December 4, 1946, he was hanged in the war criminal prison at Landsberg am Lech.

or radio, with little flags. We were on the retreat in Africa and Stalingrad had been encircled since the end of November 1942. The winter had always been advantageous for the Russians. And so I hoped that there would be a German counteroffensive in the spring and summer that would turn the tide again.

My call-up soon came rolling in. I was directed to report to the SS Signals Replacement Battalion at the SS barracks in Nuremberg at the Dutzendteich for training as a radio operator. I was assigned to the 6th Company with about 150 other young recruits. I also spent my eighteenth birthday there on February 17, 1943. Several packages arrived from home and relatives and I was happy.

The training was divided into specialized radio training and basic military training. We marched singing through the nearby fields and were instructed in how to walk like a soldier and the awe the recruits should have for their instructors and instructor assistants. Completely soaked and dirty, we marched back to the barracks with a martial song on our lips. After once again falling in, lining up and finally being dismissed, we then had to clean our clothes. The next day we were supposed to put them on dry. Unfortunately, how this was possible was not contained in the army manual. Then in the evening the duty officer inspected our quarters. The food was reasonably good, but could not compare to mother's. Weapons training—theory and practice with the Model P08 pistol, the Karabiner 98k (short) and the MG-34 light machine-gun. We had to disassemble, reassemble, explain, oil and remove oil, clean, and present in all possible situations. Line up, march, and a "masquerade ball" if something went wrong [*Translator's note:* a type of harassment favored by some instructors, in which the men were made to repeatedly appear in different dress.]. The latter was the only harassment which kindled anger and disappointment in us. We also learned to salute while standing and marching. Songs were practiced: "It is so beautiful to be a soldier," "Oh, you lovely Westerwald," or "The SS marches into enemy territory."

Radio training included getting to know the various receivers in the long-wave, short-wave, and VHF frequency ranges. Of course we also had to learn how to use the transmitters, which began at five watts and for normal units ended at about one hundred watts. The number of watts was an indicator of the transmitter's range to the next receiver. The smaller the unit, the smaller was the transmitter, for the superior units (e.g., the battalion or regiment) were deployed in the vicinity around the company. While the more powerful devices were always divided into a transmitter and a receiver, the small backpack radios combined a transmitter and receiver in one case. These devices were battery powered and were carried in one or two loads by one or two soldiers. The sets weighed more than forty pounds and with a maximum transmitting power of two watts had a range of three to fifteen miles. This in part depended on the nature of the terrain in which the equipment was used. In the mountains it was always less than on a level surface. For the one hundred-watt transmitters this was at best up to a range of 120 miles in stationary applications. Two sources of power were necessary: a 1,000-volt high-voltage source and a twelve-volt low-voltage one. The transmitter was normally installed in a *Kfz. 15* and had a lower voltage, causing performance to drop to a transmitting range of up to thirty miles. Radio training was not uninteresting and I would like to say that it was also quite demanding. Somehow operating a radio was the forerunner of today's mobile telephones.

At the end of March 1943—I had been an SS radio operator for about eight weeks—I suddenly developed fever, chills, and began to vomit. My throat became very red and my tonsils were badly swollen. I got a whitish coating on my tongue and had great difficulty swallowing. Finally I got pinhead-size red spots in my armpits and groin. Then on March 31, 1943, I was transferred to the SS hospital in Nuremberg and was placed in quarantine for six weeks. I had scarlet fever. Not until May 15, 1943, was I released from the SS hospital to join the SS Signals Replacement Battalion—my comrades,

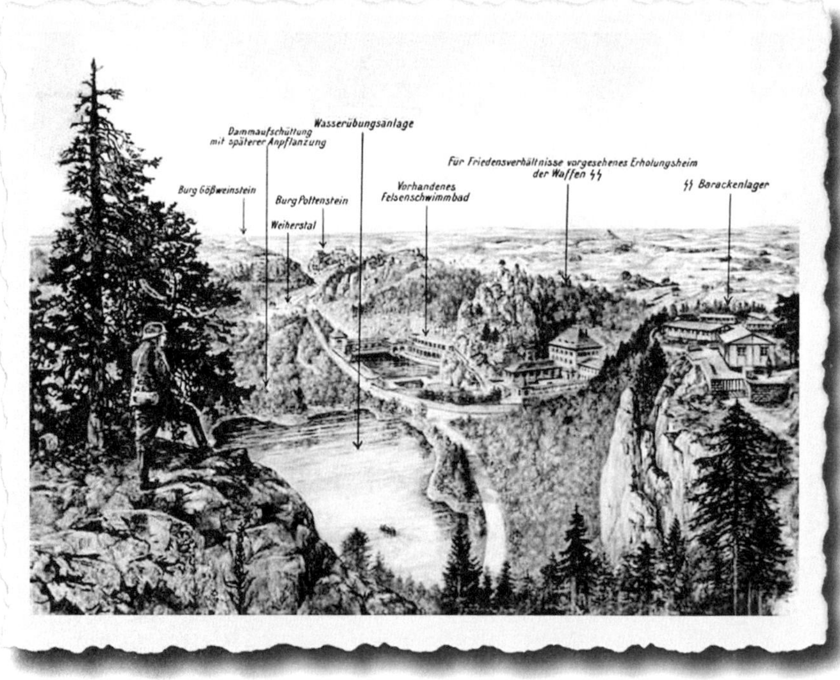

This drawing by *SS-Standartenführer* Dr. Brand shows the existing and planned installations of the *Karstwehr* Training Facility in Pottenstein. In addition to the historic castles of Gößweinstein and Pottenstein, it points to the water training area, the swimming pool and the SS barracks camp.

The barracks of the *SS-Karstwehr-Bataillon* in Pottenstein.

Below: The multi-purpose room.

Engineers and mountain troops training in the Pottenstein karst.

however, had all meanwhile been transferred to field units. Actually I was supposed to have gone to the *SS-Panzergrenadier-Division "Hitler Jugend"* then being formed.

So at first I remained in Nuremberg, and then four weeks later, on June 18, 1943, I left for the French training camp at Rennes to join the *SS-Sturmbrigade "Reichsführer-SS."* My immune system was not yet back to normal, however, for no sooner had I gotten over the scarlet fever when I began having difficulty swallowing again. I was constantly nauseous and I had pain in my abdomen and limbs. I developed fever and an unpleasant odor came from my mouth. I had come down with diphtheria. And so it was back to the hospital, where I stayed until June 23, 1943. Once again I had missed out on a field unit. When I was finally healthy again, on June 30, 1943, I and two comrades from the SS Signals Replacement Battalion—*SS-Sturmmann* Siegler and *SS-Funker* Schöning—received transfer orders to the Headquarters Company of the *SS-Karstwehr-Bataillon* in Pottenstein.

Chapter 2
With the *SS-Karstwehr-Bataillon*

Of the three of us, none had ever heard of an *SS-Karstwehr-Bataillon* and so during our train ride we deliberated as to what kind of unit it could be. On arriving in Pottenstein we asked our way through to our new unit's quarters. Pottenstein was an idyllic small town built mostly on both sides of a country road. At the eastern end of the town there was a man-made pond, the so-called pioneer water training area, and a Felsenbad. Just behind it, one went up the mountain to a wooden barracks camp in which the battalion was housed. We ultimately learned that it was a special unit of the *Reichsführer-SS* which was supposed to be trained for special actions in karst regions. They told us that the battalion was originally supposed to be used to take Malta or deployed somewhere in the Caucasus Mountains. That was something.

Our battalion commander was *SS-Standartenführer* Professor Dr. Brand, a well-known cave explorer. He was already more than sixty years old and visually he resembled what small children imagine a "good uncle" to be. Dr. Brand had, I believe, become a teacher and he was more like a grandfather to us than a strict superior. The battalion had been in Pottenstein for a year and had carried out cave training, mountain climbing, and other things associated with mountain troops.

I was assigned to the Headquarters Company's signals platoon, which was led by *SS-Sturmscharführer* Ferenzky, who had been a soldier in the *Reichswehr*. I remember the comrades *SS-Oberscharführer* Weiß, *SS-Unterscharführer* Gallenschütz, Linsmair, Rödel, and *SS-Rottenführer* Schanz, Bechert, Stock, Astor, and Weblek, as well as

SS-Sturmmann Funke and *SS-Funker* Tonsor.

The signals platoon was organized into:

1 section group
1 motorized field telephone team (1 *Kfz. 15*)
1 motorized radio team (1 *Kfz. 15*)
3 backpack radio teams (mounted)
1 field telephone team (mounted)
1 signals equipment vehicle (horse-drawn)
and its authorized strength was 1 officer, and 29 other ranks, and 25 horses.

While the infantry were tormented in the field every day, we new radio operators had normal duty plus two or three radio exercises. Many were given leave and those who remained were sent to help the surrounding farmers bring in the harvest.

After the Allies landed in Sicily on July 10, 1943, beginning the battle for Fortress Europe, it was announced that we were being sent to Italy. We knew nothing about the political situation. Until the end Italy was portrayed as a loyal partner in the so-called Pact of Steel. As is so often the case, the reality was much different. On July 12, 1943, we boarded trains in Pegnitz, spent the night in Treuchtlingen about fifty-five miles away, and at 2245 the next evening we detrained in Mühlbach on the Hochkönig (approximately five miles southwest of Werfens) in what was then Ostmark (Austria). From Treuchtlingen we had travelled about 150 miles in freight cars bedded with straw.

From Mühlbach station we marched to a barracks camp near the Birgkarhaus. We remained there for about three weeks, and the headquarters company was supposed to ensure cooperation between all the units of the battalion. Everything worked extremely well, however, and there were no complaints from anyone. About half the members of the battalion were Reich Germans and the other half were ethnic Germans from Rumania, but they were excellent chaps, true comrades. We trained hard, sometimes with live firing, and exercises were held. The food was good, which helped keep morale high. Of course rumors circulated as to what we were doing there and what our ultimate operational objective was. We surely had our eye on a move to Italy though. We asked our company commanders, but they shrouded themselves in silence. Either they didn't know themselves or had been ordered to maintain secrecy. I believe that our superiors themselves had no idea and racked their brains as to what the future would bring.

When the Italian Duce—Benito Mussolini—was deposed during a sitting of the Grand Fascist Council and arrested, new discussions began among us. Was this the reason we had been moved to the border? The new prime minister was Marshall Pietro Badoglio, who declared on the radio that the war on the side of the Axis would continue. But why then had they deposed Mussolini? Were we to help stabilize the situation in Italy? On August 9, 1943, our *SS-Karstwehr-Bataillon* marched into Bischofshofen, which was about seven miles away, and there we boarded trains. Again our destination was a mystery. Our company commander told us, however, that we were supposed to secure important traffic junctions in the border region. In fact we arrived in Villach on August 11, 1943. The closer we got to the Italian border, the more German troops we saw in and around the villages. This made it clear to me that we would probably soon be crossing into Italy. Because of the many units, accommodations were often extended to private quarters. The food was good, as was morale.

After three days in Villach, on August 14, 1943, we again moved farther in the direction of the Italian border. In Arnoldstein, six miles from Villach, we were less than a mile from the German–Italian border, and there we set up a telephone exchange between German agencies.

My comrades and I took up quarters in a barn in the center of

Arnoldstein. Lice, fleas, and other vermin were a plague day and night. Our activities there were limited to drill and servicing weapons and equipment. Barely two weeks later—on August 26, 1943—we marched out of Arnoldstein in the direction of the Italian border, which we crossed shortly after one in the afternoon.

We initially camped in Tarvis, in Italian territory just a mile beyond the border. Our battalion bivouacked in tents and then on August 27, 1943, marched into Pontebba, which was about nine miles away. We were quartered with South Tyrolean families and they received us with unbelievable warmth and hospitality. Omelets made with four or more eggs and excellent ham were normal. There was also South Tyrolean wine to drink. Wonderful.

Our march continued without incident. We reached Moggio Udinese about nine miles away and were housed in the local gymnasium. The residents were not real South Tyroleans and were rather reserved towards us. I would not like to say that they were cool, but one could not say that they welcomed us. The next day we marched back to Camporosso. The command post with our commanding officer Dr. Brand and the entire staff was set up in the Gasthof Post. Today this inn is completely run down.

We were quartered in haylofts in the center of town. Outside of town there was an Alpini (Italian mountain troops) barracks and not far from our quarters there was also an Italian police strongpoint with approximately forty Carabinieri. We had contact with our Italian allies. We saluted each other and when we could we chatted with them. We did wonder, however, why the Italians always had their weapons on them—even when they went to church!

At about 2200 on the night of September 8–9, 1943, our platoon leader came and informed us that the disarming and internment of the Italians was going to begin the next morning. Of course we were all very surprised and excited. Sleep was out of the question and at best we dozed a little. Preparations began at about two in the morning and after the Italians allowed an ultimatum to surrender expire, at four in the morning we attacked. The Italians had obviously received orders not to allow themselves to be disarmed without a fight, and we immediately came under heavy return fire. Several comrades and I lay near a railway underpass, which was about 150 feet from the Carabinieri strongpoint.

When we were finally joined by several SS officers from the headquarters staff, the Alpini began shooting at us with mortars and heavy machine-guns. The outburst went on for about thirty to forty minutes, then it suddenly grew quiet. The Carabinieri and some of the Alpini approached with hands raised. They were rounded up and in the yard of the Gasthof Post readied for transport out. The Italians were not treated as the enemy. Unarmed officers and other ranks stood among us and were probably not very unhappy that the war for them was now over. Our battalion commander had a long conversation with the Alpini colonel, who puffed away on a cigarette. Our signals platoon finally took over the small Carabinieri strongpoint.

In the nights that followed, shots were sometimes fired when the Alpini who had fled into the mountain came back down into the valley. To prevent unpleasant surprises, we barricaded our quarters, but we were happy when our battalion's motor pool moved to Camporosso. Our battalion was not deployed in just one village, instead it was divided among several.

After the arrival of our vehicles we had quite considerable firepower. We took our turn guarding the command post in the Gasthof Post. We stood guard there day and night, and apart from several minor incidents not much happened. Now and again our commanding officer *SS-Standartenführer* "Papa" Brand would come out of the inn in the morning and pass us some alcohol: "To warm up!" as he put it. It was not unusual for him to hug us young boys and ask: "Son, did you have a good night?" He was a considerate old gentleman who had a big heart for his young subordinates. We liked him very much.

It also wasn't so bad that he and the headquarters staff slept in made beds, while we lived with fleas, mice, and rats. We had set up a switchboard with about twenty connections in the Carabinieri quarters and kept it constantly manned. As well, so-called backpack radio teams were attached to the various companies, which were supposed to secure the Flitscher Klause–Karfreit (where Erwin Rommel had fought in the First World War) –Tolmein area across the Predil Pass in the Italian-Slovenian border region.

After the victorious Balkan Campaign in 1941, Slovenia had been divided among Germany, Italy, and Hungary. Everywhere resistance against the occupiers developed quickly. While Germany and Hungary carried out a quite restrictive policy against Slovenian nationalism and of course the communists who were there, Italy was incapable of effectively dealing with the Slovenian partisans. As a result, a relatively strong partisan army was able to develop in the former Slovenian areas of the Italian province of Görz and it eventually came under strong influence from Tito.

The first mission given our *SS-Karstwehr-Bataillon* therefore was to free the important traffic routes and lines of communication in the province of Görz. It was in this area on the Isonzo River in 1917 that the 12th Battle of Isonzo had been fought—specifically for Karfreit (Kobarid in Slovenian and Caporetto in Italian). Erwin Rommel, who later rose to the rank of *Generalfeldmarschall*, was awarded the *Pour le Mérite* for his actions there.

I was detached to the 3rd Company, which placed me under company commander *SS-Obersturmführer* Scheid. A former member of the *SS-Heimwehr Danzig*, he wore the cuff title with the same name on the left sleeve of his tunic. *SS-Obersturmführer* Scheid was an elegant and good superior, who met a tragic fate. On September 20, 1943, we climbed into the truck and drove through the idyllic Predil Pass past old customs and border posts and mountain lakes, constantly on guard in case we came under fire. A comrade and I sat together in *SS-Obersturmführer* Scheid's car, in case that some

SS-Standartenführer Dr. Hans Brand commanded the *SS-Karstwehr-Bataillon* until March 23, 1944.

Left: *SS-Standartenführer* Dr. Brand with *SS-Untersturmführer* Kühbandner in Pottenstein.

Below: *SS-Standartenführer* Dr. Brand with his adjutant, *SS-Obersturmführer* Weiland, in the area of operations in the spring of 1944.

sort of report might have to be passed on immediately. The company commander sat in the passenger seat next to the driver, making a total of four persons in the vehicle.

As we neared Flitsch (Bovec in Slovenian and Plezzo in Italian) from the north, we came under heavy fire from the Flitscher Klause. The Flitscher Klause was a small fortress at the bridge over the Koritnica Gorge, approximately 2.5 miles northwest of Flitsch. It had been built in the late nineteenth century to prevent Italian troops from breaking through the Koritnica Valley and the Predil Pass to Austria. We were facing Slovenian partisans who felt that their previous quiet had been disturbed. Scheid had us get out immediately and we spread out. I had the heavy backpack radio on my back and tried to remain close to the *Obersturmführer*. Then he ordered me to contact battalion and request air support. In the meantime another of our companies approached and occupied an assembly area for the imminent attack. Before very long three or four dive bombers appeared. They dropped their bombs and we began the assault. The partisans ran like hares and we secured the area.

Then we got into the vehicles again and drove toward the town of Flitsch. There too we were welcomed by bursts of machine-gun fire. As this was no fortified town, the units immediately stormed it. While we did have casualties, I believe that the partisans were very impressed or even shocked by our appearance and action. They had never seen anything like it from the Italian security forces. We broke into the town, and after the first street and house fighting the partisans withdrew. We then began checking the remaining population to determine if they lived there or were from elsewhere. The latter were suspected to be partisans.

Meanwhile other parts of the battalion had arrived, taking charge of the wounded and reinforcing us. The partisans were not pursued, and actually these initial actions accomplished little. The partisans that had gotten away hid in the surrounding villages and forests and were not destroyed. It was like swimming in a lake overgrown with

Wilfried Sonnethal (second from left) as a member of a backpack radio team.

A "partisan shelter" is burned to the ground.

Checking the population of a village during an operation.

algae. The algae was pushed away as one swam through it, but then closed in again behind one. Nevertheless, we always displayed presence and determination.

The next-largest town—Saga—was also occupied by partisans and it was more or less a partisan stronghold. Here, too, there was fierce fighting with the insurgents. We came to realize that all of Slovenia—at least the part seceded to Italy—was completely controlled or infiltrated by the partisans.

It was clear that special operations would have to be planned and carried out to help remedy this problem. And so on October 6, 1943, we were again sent into the upper Isonzo Valley together with two companies of the 139th Mountain Infantry Replacement and Training Regiment. And once again there was heavy fighting which ended in the partisans withdrawing. We initially secured the area and then advanced further. As far as our strength permitted, we tried to find partisans and Italian soldiers in hiding. We repeatedly fought large and small engagements. Places identified as harboring partisans were destroyed, usually burned down.

On October 31, 1943, we met fierce resistance on the hills in front of Karfreit (Kobarid in Slovenian and Caporetto in Italian). Partisans manning three bunkers fired Italian machine guns at us. We had no mortars and so *SS-Obersturmführer* Scheid ordered the bunkers taken out with concentrated charges—clusters of hand grenade charges tied around a single handle. Three comrades cautiously crept or crawled from the sides towards the enemy bunkers, which were made of tree trunks, pulled the cord at the end of the wooden handle and threw the charges in the direction of the embrasures. Seconds later they exploded with a huge noise. The logs and countless wood splinters flew through the air and the other comrades charged.

Many partisans were killed and others were taken prisoner. We pressed on to Karfreit, where we were fired at from almost every house. We nevertheless were able to take the fiercely-defended town.

The next night the partisans launched several counterattacks and there were in fact supposed to have been about 800 insurgents there. We had been reinforced by mortars and heavy machine guns of our 4th Company and put the Slovenians to flight.

Not long afterward we received news by radio that members of the police were almost encircled and that we were to relieve them. Scheid had the company fall in immediately and we rapidly marched off. It wasn't long before we began taking fire from a village. The *SS-Obersturmführer* was certainly not one to risk the lives of his men, but he obviously thought that storming the village was the only option. While I, with the forty-five-pound load on my back, panted after the company some distance behind, the rest of the company had deployed for the attack and began storming the village. Once again the Slovenian partisans withdrew quickly. One could almost believe that Scheid was right, for the partisans had always run from an energetic attack. But this time he wasn't right. We got near to our endangered police comrades, but then we were ourselves attacked and forced to pull back. This was a bitter disappointment, especially because we heard the sound of combat from the encircled police but saw nothing more. We had several wounded, which I reported to the battalion by radio. Battalion told us to assume an all-round defense position, it would send reinforcements. We then defended ourselves in our hedgehog for about six hours, and after the partisans broke off the engagement we were able to withdraw through a small hamlet and eventually got all of our wounded safely back to battalion. I do not know what became of the police, but I assume that they were rescued by other units and that is the reason why the insurgents attacking us suddenly withdrew.

We spent several days in the Karfreit area, in bivouac. During a subsequent action there we came under heavy machine-gun fire from a house. Several comrades worked their way up to it and set it on fire. Then the house was stormed. The partisans left many dead and wounded behind and escaped through the rear windows. They didn't get far, however. We advanced further, towards Tolmein (Tolmin in Slovenian, and Tolmino in Italian). On November 4, 1943, we reached Volzana, to its south. We moved along the Isonzo, south through Santa Lucia.

Then we moved back to the north and were deployed on the Montemaggiore. There and farther below there was already under snow and our pack animals could go no farther. So we had to carry our equipment and ammunition ourselves. It was a slog. As well it was bitter cold and in bivouac we froze with no end. Once we stopped an attempted breakthrough by the partisans with just one light machine gun and a few rifles. Another time I stayed with the numerous wounded and talked with them until a truck came and took them away under fire. Once we were supposed to approach a village from the left, but suddenly we ourselves came under fire from a wood about fifty meters away on our flank. We took cover and lobbed hand grenades at the wood. Then we attacked it. Our men immediately began working their way towards the enemy strongpoint which was placing the dangerous flanking fire on our advancing elements. The enemy was eliminated with hand grenade clusters.

On November 27, 1943, we had a very nice social evening in relatively far away Veldes (Slovenian Bled, approximately twelve miles east of Triglav). There was singing and laughing, music played, and we ate and drank. We remembered our dead and wounded and really felt ourselves something special. In any case we didn't feel inferior and thought that we would soon put an end to the bandits (partisans).

On December 1, 1943, we entrained in Feistritz, about nine miles away, and were taken via Assling to Sagrado–Gradisca. There we were sent to an empty Italian barracks in Gradisca. There our military routine continued exactly as per normal, with drill, rifle drill, marching, etc.

On December 18, 1943, I received my annual leave. I travelled by truck in very moderate temperatures to Tarvis and from there by train to Württemberg. I took a bus from Heilbronn to my hometown and then walked home. Just before midnight I was back with my parents and our joy at being reunited was great. Unfortunately, I again had problems with my health. I spent Christmas with my parents, again with a very bad sore throat, fever, and chills. The day after Christmas I went to Heilbronn and entered the reserve hospital in the seminary.

As I could myself detect a rather unpleasant odor from my mouth, I rightly feared that I had infected tonsils again. The staff doctor in the hospital found the lymph nodes in my neck were swollen and suspected that I had abscessed tonsils. I remained in the hospital until January 5, 1944, and was given anti-inflammatory drugs. My condition improved and I was released from the hospital. I was given fourteen days recovery leave, which I spent with my parents. Unfortunately, my joy was short lived and my condition again deteriorated rapidly. I reported back to the reserve hospital in Heilbronn on January 21, 1944. The abscess had by then progressed so far that they decided on surgical intervention (tonsillectomy). I felt terrible. I stayed in the hospital in Heilbronn until February 11, 1944, and was then given another fourteen days recovery leave.

As neither I nor the hospital had reported my illness and operation to the *SS-Karstwehr-Bataillon*, my parents had already received a visit from the military police. The battalion had initially reported me "absent without leave" and finally as "deserted." The military police had thus gone to my home while I was in the hospital and asked where I was. They were ready to take me away in handcuffs, but my mother explained where I was and a member of the military police turned up at the Heilbronn Reserve Hospital in the seminary. While he stood by my bed, I had to show him my pay book and at least in this respect the matter was solved. My state of health, however, was still poor.

Left: *SS-Sturmmann* Wilfried Sonnenthal in the spring of 1944.

Below: On the far left with members of the Signals Platoon.

After again recovering at home for the next fourteen days, on February 28, 1944, I took leave of my parents and travelled back to my unit, which was still in Gradisca – Sagrado, by way of Heilbronn, the Brenner Pass, and Verona. There I was promoted to *SS-Sturmmann* retroactive to February 1, 1944.

Our actions went on. Partly by rail transport but mainly by truck, we were moved as deep as possible into the area of operations. Not just our weapons and ammunition, but also our rations and also our mules were transported in the vehicles. Sometimes there were twenty to thirty men standing on the beds of the trucks. Then the trucks were unloaded—often under fire from the partisans—and we went into the mountains.

In addition to mules we also had horses, which as a rule were used by the pack animal sections. *SS-Unterscharführer* Rathke was the battalion's feed master and was also responsible for caring for the animals. As he was a trained farmer, he not only had the necessary knowledge but also the desire. When the vehicles could go no farther, the horses and mules were used to transport supplies (especially food and ammunition).

Almost all of our operations were given code names to fool enemy intelligence. My first action after returning from leave and illness was "Operation Cypress," which lasted three days, from March 3–5, 1944. It was a small action just a few miles from our quarters in Gradisca. Although it was not far away, as usual during such operations we spent the night in the operational area. If barns were available we slept there, if not in a tent bivouac.

That same month I took part in "Operations Mole" and "Pale Blue." These operations took place in the Komen area, about nine miles southeast of Gradisca, where there was an especially heavy concentration of partisans. Once, parts of two companies were approaching the supply train coming from Gradisca, when they suddenly came under heavy enemy fire. The comrades immediately set up a machine-gun and covered their withdrawal to the unit. The supply train was warned and withdrew to Gradisca. We had no casualties, but we also had nothing to eat that evening.

That same month we were deployed on Monte Nero (Slovenian Krn) and cleared the once well-constructed First World War positions of partisans. From there we drove from Zacreio Pass through Rauna di Dresenva (Slovenian Drezniske Ravne) to Karfreit. *SS-Obersturmführer* Ernst Scheid also led us very well through the difficult limestone formations of the Julian high mountain karst and we played a significant part in clearing the important Flitsch–Karfreit–Cividale telephone cable line. *SS-Obersturmführer* Scheid was awarded the Iron Cross, First Class for this action in March 1944. He had previously been awarded the Iron Cross, Second Class on November 9, 1943.

"Operation Dachstein" (Roof Tile), which began on March 25, 1944, took us into Ternov Forest (Trnovski Gozd in Slovenian, Selva di Tarnova in Italian), which was just nine miles northeast of Komen. This was a large operation in which at least two police regiments took part in addition to our battalion. When we attacked a heavily-fortified hill position, we again came under heavy fire. While everyone returned fire, I ran back and brought up ammunition for the machine-gunners, who were almost out of ammunition. The position was taken, along with two others and a village behind them. The fighting was becoming increasingly difficult. In the beginning one only had to launch an assault to put the enemy to flight, but this was no longer the case. We had to be carefully not to get a bloody nose ourselves.

"Operation Osterglocke" (Easter Bell) ran from March 31 to April 11, 1944. In conjunction with units of the police and the *Wehrmacht*, this time we were supposed to clear the Istrian Peninsula of partisans in the area southeast of Trieste, sweeping from north to south. We combed the area but had almost no contact with the enemy. Not until the last evening did we find a large concentration of partisans near the town of Pedena. The 3rd Company split up

SS-Hauptsturmführer Berschneider, commander of the *SS-Karstwehr-Bataillon*.

The battalion assembled for a speech by the Senior SS and Police Commander.

Speech by *SS-Gruppenführer und General der Polizei* Odilo Globocnik, Senior SS and Police Commander "Adriatic Coastland."

The *SS-Karstwehr-Bataillon* took part in the parade in Trieste on April 20, 1944, Hitler's birthday.

into platoons and attacked from different sides. The fighting went on into the night, when the partisans withdrew. We had uncovered and destroyed a partisan nest. But what did that mean? The partisans were receiving generous support from Great Britain and an ever greater inflow from the population and the Croatian partisan leader Tito succeeded in turning uncoordinated and barely fit-for-action units into capable formations. Everywhere we went we saw slogans in Slovenian painted on the walls: *"Zivel Tito"* – *"Zivel Tovaris Stalin"* – *"Zivil Partizane"* – *Zivela Rdeca Armada"* (Long Live Tito – Long Live Comrade Stalin – Long Live the Partisans – Long Live the Red Army).

Back in Gradisca there followed intensive formal training: drill with rifles and marching, fall in and line up, etc. The battalion was ordered to Trieste for the April 20, 1944, to take part in a parade to mark Hitler's birthday. We assembled in side streets in front of the Palace of Justice and then marched towards it past dignitaries such as Friedrich Rainer, Gauleiter of Carinthia, or *SS-Gruppenführer* Odilo Globocnik, Senior SS and Police Commander in the Adriatic Coastland area of operations. The parade was led by the Senior SS and Police Commander's motorized SS and police units and behind them marched numerous German SS and police formations. We were in the forward third and marched like tin soldiers through the streets and positioned ourselves in the assigned sectors in front of the Palace of Justice. Behind us came Italian and Slovenian volunteer units, trying hard to look smart, but this only made us laugh. For we knew the mentality of our allies: pompous as long as there was no shooting, and when the action did start they disappeared as quickly as they could!

The large-scale "Operation Braunschweig" (Brunswick) began in Istria in the last week of April and continued until May 6, 1944. As always, as part of the backpack radio team I was attached to the company headquarters squad and was near the company commander. We reported by radio to battalion when we had reached the day's

Members of the Signals Platoon – above in barracks in Gradisca (Wilfried Sonnenthal is fourth from left), and below ready for action (Wilfried Sonnenthal is second from right).

objectives, when something out of the ordinary happened, or for example when we met strong enemy resistance requiring support. From battalion we received changes in plans of operation, received objectives of the day, and were informed about special occurrences or events affecting neighboring units or other companies. In addition to radio duty we usually also guarded the command post—our radio team's equipment also included a light machine-gun.

After "Operation Brunswick" we were put aboard trains and taken back to Gradisca. There we were given several days rest. *SS-Standartenführer* Professor Dr. Brand, our former commanding officer, left on May 13, 1944. He was too old to lead an active unit against partisans and he had not been present for our most recent actions. Our new commanding officer was *SS-Hauptsturmführer* Berschneider. He was a native of the Upper Pfalz and he had actually led the battalion for some time already. It was a sad scene when Professor Dr. Brand—who was a very fine man who we called "Papa" Brand—bowed to the rather boyish *SS-Gruppenführer* Globocnik, the Senior SS and Police Commander in the Adriatic Coastland area of operations, during the farewell ceremony. The thought went through my head that it was like an animal thanking the butcher that he is about to be slaughtered.

"Operation Liane" followed from May 22–24, 1944. It was a sweep of the Casteldobra area, approximately twelve miles north of our base in Gradisca. This was followed by "Operation Annemarie" from June 7–16, 1944, in which we again marched into the Trieste area by way of Görz. We were supposed to make contact with police units there. We did not find them, however, but we suddenly came under heavy fire and hid in a barn for the night. We were about to leave the next morning when two partisans entered the barn. We knocked them out with rifle butt blows to the skull. Soon afterwards another twenty to twenty-five partisans appeared and we opened up on them from only thirty feet away. Half of them were cut down, the others ran away and returned with two light machine-guns. We slipped out the back of the barn and came to a slope, but we soon came under fire. Ducking our heads, we ran down the slope backwards and hid in the bushes. We then spent the night there, with almost no ammunition. Avoiding roads and paths, we even removed our mountain boots so as not to make any noise. With sore feet, hungry and thirsty, after swimming a river we reached a German strongpoint. Gone were the days when the partisans ran away like greyhounds. Now it was we who ran.

Things did not always go the enemy's way, however. Once we were sweeping a forest and without warning came upon partisans. We immediately opened fire and charged the partisans. We clearly had the element of surprise on our side.

That was the end of active anti-partisan operations by our *SS-Karstwehr-Bataillon*. We were supposed to be expanded into a division and for this purpose were transferred to Tolmezzo, approximately thirty-five miles to the north. We wondered about this, for we were only a battalion and were immediately supposed to be expanded into a division with a total of about fourteen battalions. How was that possible? Actually all of the soldiers of our battalion were supposed to be used as instructors for newly-drafted recruits. Only the 2nd Company under *SS-Obersturmführer* Kühbandner was divided into hunting detachments. Wearing civilian clothes most of the time, it tried to conduct reconnaissance in our quartering area and cause unrest among the partisans and partisan sympathizers.

I was given about twenty South Tyrolean youths, and I as a nineteen-year-old was supposed to instruct them in the field of radio. They sent us everything that was available to bring the division up to authorized strength. In addition to about 500 South Tyroleans we received Spaniards, who pedaled through Tolmezzo on "organized" bicycles beneath open umbrellas for protection against the blazing sun. That was a bizarre picture. A small Albanian was assigned to me as a pack animal leader. There were also Italians, who had obviously been forcefully conscripted and had almost no motivation

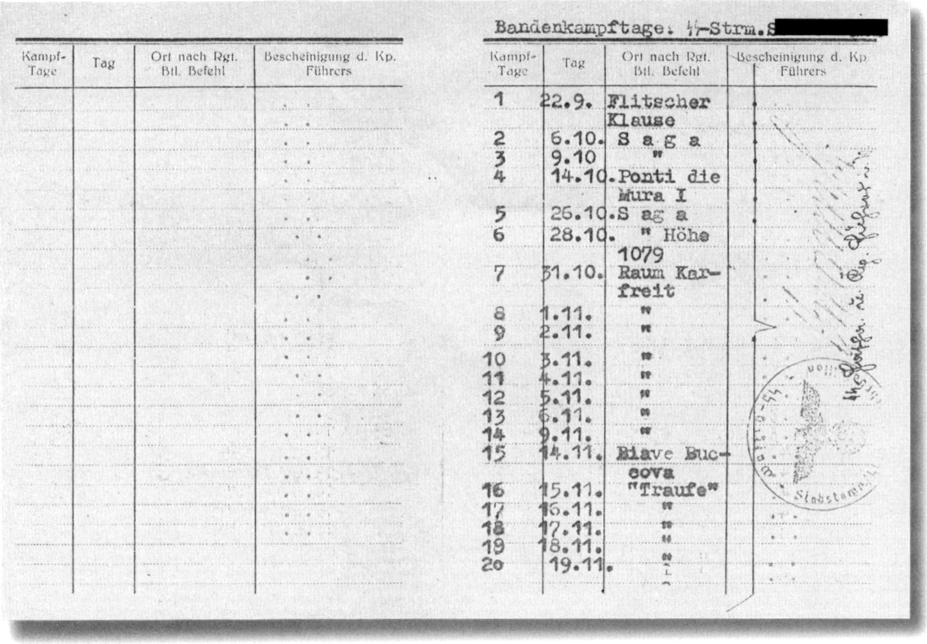

Kampf-Tage	Tag	Ort nach Rgt. Btl. Befehl	Bescheinigung d. Kp. Führers

Bandenkampftage: ϟϟ-Strm. S[redacted]

Kampf-Tage	Tag	Ort nach Rgt. Btl. Befehl	Bescheinigung d. Kp. Führers
1	22.9.	Flitscher Klause	
2	6.10.	S a g a	
3	9.10	"	
4	14.10.	Ponti die Mura I	
5	26.10.	S ag a	
6	28.10.	" Höhe 1079	
7	31.10.	Raum Karfreit	
8	1.11.	"	
9	2.11.	"	
10	3.11.	"	
11	4.11.	"	
12	5.11.	"	
13	6.11.	"	
14	9.11.	"	
15	14.11.	Biave Buccova	
16	15.11.	"Traufe"	
17	16.11.	"	
18	17.11.	"	
19	18.11.	"	
20	19.11.	"	

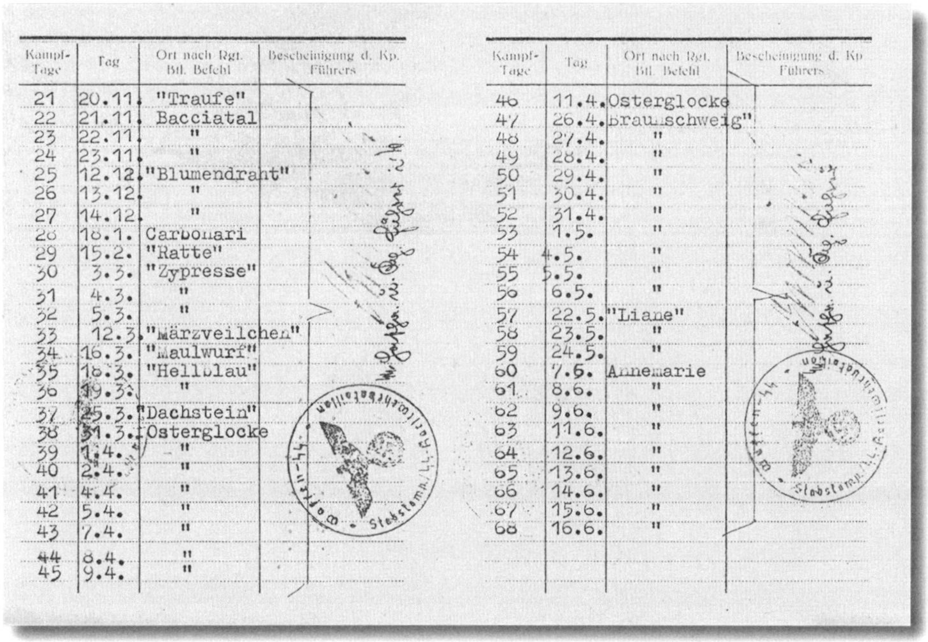

Kampf-Tage	Tag	Ort nach Rgt. Btl. Befehl	Bescheinigung d. Kp. Führers
21	20.11.	"Traufe"	
22	21.11.	Bacciatal	
23	22.11.	"	
24	23.11.	"	
25	12.12.	"Blumendraht"	
26	13.12.	"	
27	14.12.	"	
28	18.1.	Carbonari	
29	15.2.	"Ratte"	
30	3.3.	"Zypresse"	
31	4.3.	"	
32	5.3.	"	
33	12.3.	"Märzveilchen"	
34	16.3.	"Maulwurf"	
35	18.3.	"Hellblau"	
36	19.3.	"	
37	25.3.	"Dachstein"	
38	31.3.	Osterglocke	
39	1.4.	"	
40	2.4.	"	
41	4.4.	"	
42	5.4.	"	
43	7.4.	"	
44	8.4.	"	
45	9.4.	"	

Kampf-Tage	Tag	Ort nach Rgt. Btl. Befehl	Bescheinigung d. Kp. Führers
46	11.4.	Osterglocke	
47	26.4.	Braunschweig"	
48	27.4.	"	
49	28.4.	"	
50	29.4.	"	
51	30.4.	"	
52	31.4.	"	
53	1.5.	"	
54	4.5.	"	
55	5.5.	"	
56	6.5.	"	
57	22.5.	"Liane"	
58	23.5.	"	
59	24.5.	"	
60	7.6.	Annemarie	
61	8.6.	"	
62	9.6.	"	
63	11.6.	"	
64	12.6.	"	
65	13.6.	"	
66	14.6.	"	
67	15.6.	"	
68	16.6.	"	

Wilfried Sonnenthal's paybook records sixty-six partisan combat days by June 16, 1944. He did not take part in a number of them, however, and did not see any close combat. He nevertheless received the Anti-Partisan War Badge in Bronze.

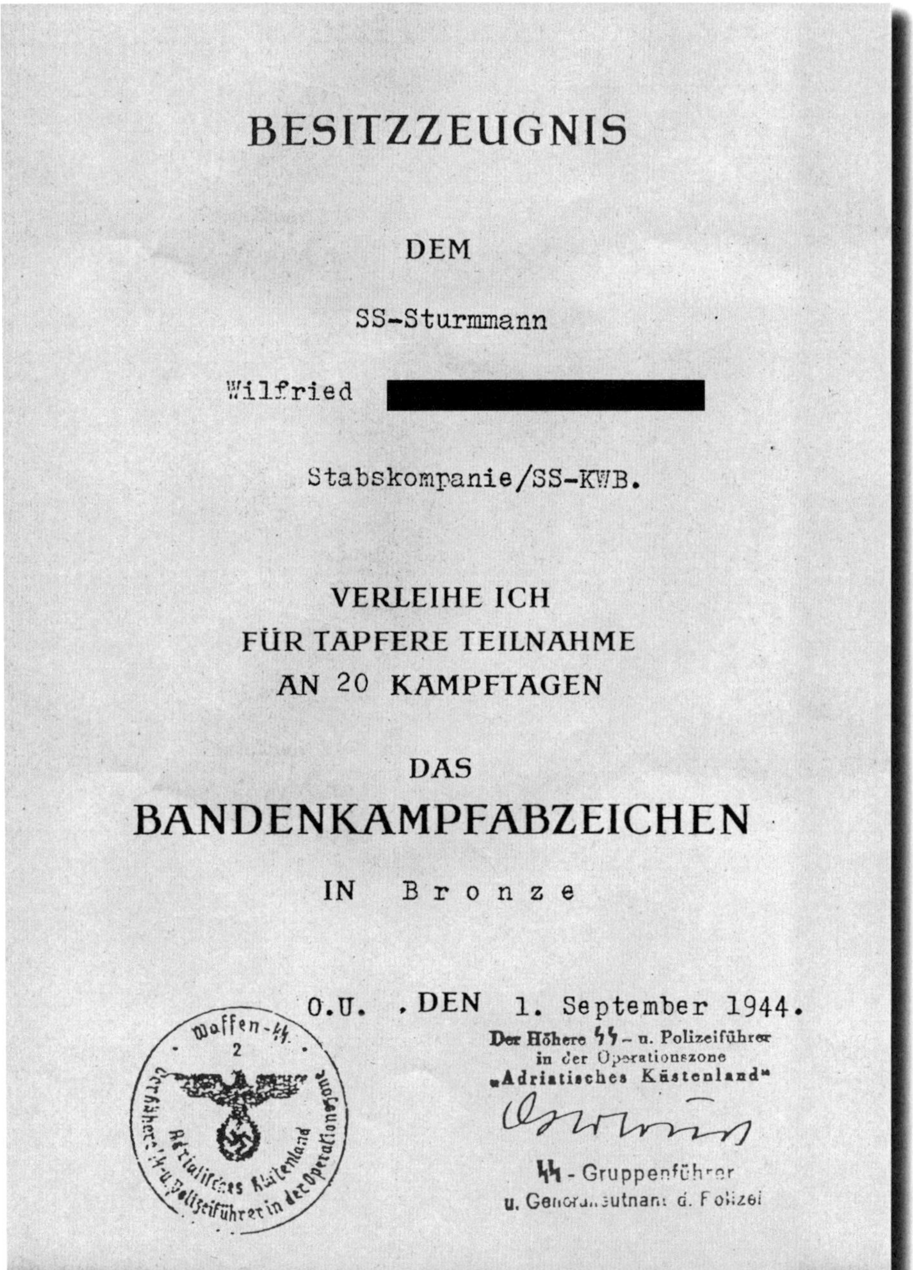

BESITZZEUGNIS

DEM

SS-Sturmmann

Wilfried [redacted]

Stabskompanie/SS-KWB.

VERLEIHE ICH
FÜR TAPFERE TEILNAHME
AN 20 KAMPFTAGEN

DAS

BANDENKAMPFABZEICHEN

IN Bronze

O.U. , DEN 1. September 1944.

Der Höhere SS- u. Polizeiführer
in der Operationszone
„Adriatisches Küstenland"

SS - Gruppenführer
u. Generalleutnant d. Polizei

The award document that accompanied his Anti-Partisan War Badge in Bronze.

for what was for them very stressful duty. I also remember some Slovenians, Bosnians, and Croats. It was a multi-ethnic formation, as in the times of the Austro-Hungarian monarchy. The only ones who really wanted to be there were the South Tyroleans, but they were excellent comrades: modest and brave.

For me this meant half a year as an instructor in Tolmezzo—it was a wonderful time. In contrast to others I had only training duty. Otherwise I enjoyed the sun with comrades, drank grappa, played football, and enjoying God's blessings. There was little to no sign of the war—I almost felt as if I was on summer vacation!

In July 1944, our orderly office issued us pay book inserts on which was recorded all of our company's anti-partisan actions. We were about to be awarded the Anti-Partisan Badge. This form was probably filled out for all members of the company, in the assumption that every soldier had taken part on all of the company's actions. So my insert also included actions that took place when I wasn't even in Italy but in the hospital in Heilbronn.

Other, more precise information seemed to be on the other side, for when I became one of the first ones to be awarded the Anti-Partisan Badge in Tolmezzo on September 1, 1944, I only received the Anti-Partisan Badge in Bronze for twenty action days. However, sixty-eight combat days were already recorded in my pay book insert for the period from September 1943 to mid-June 1944. This list contained all of the company's actions which resulted in hostilities with the partisans. In fact only close combat days were supposed to be recorded, meaning days when we had seen the whites of the enemy's eyes. These were very rare moments for me, and consequently I probably shouldn't have been awarded the anti-partisan badge. But it was probably recognition of my actions as a radio operator, and they were certainly not easier than those of the light infantry.

During the ceremonial presentation of the badges we had to form up in the square and then the names of the individual recipients were called out. We stepped forward and were then presented the certificate and the badge. Our pay books were collected and we got them back the next day stamped with the appropriate entries and signed. We celebrated the awarding in the evening by pouring grappa into a bowl and adding crackers. The crackers absorbed the grappa and we let them dissolve slowly in our mouths. Before long we were rather tight, but that was nothing unusual for Tolmezzo.

We were sent on another larger operation from November 27 to December 13, 1944. In the province of Udine we were supposed to clear partisans from an area envisaged for the construction of positions. It was "Operation Achse" (Axis) which, in addition to us, involved other German, native, and foreign units. The booty in weapons, ammunition, and supplies was considerable and it significantly improved our equipment and rations, which by then had become meager.

When *Wehrmacht* units were withdrawn from the front, partisans immediately occupied the area around the Wippach Valley near Görz. We were immediately sent against them and afterwards once again combed the Tarnov Forest. In the process we destroyed some Alpine huts and partisan camps. This caused them no serious damage.

Christmas and New Years Eve 1944, came and went. We were not exactly in low spirits, but we weren't particularly euphoric either. Our cooks still managed to prepare good meals and there were also plenty of cookies. New Years Eve saw many belts of tracer pass through our machine-guns and each man swore to himself that we would finish the partisans in the New Year.

Chapter 3
The End of the War and After

On January 30, 1945, I was promoted to *SS-Rottenführer*. I had been a soldier and member of the *Waffen-SS* for just under two years and my twentieth birthday was approaching. This I was able to celebrate with comrades over a few glasses of grappa.

On February 19, 1945, two days after my birthday, I was ordered from Tolmezzo to Pontebba. I spend fourteen days there and was then employed at our workshop in Moggio Udinese. There all of our signals equipment, transmitters, receivers, backpack radios, etc., were serviced, overhauled, or repaired. Now I was no telecommunications engineer, who knew all about such things. I could operate the equipment, but I knew nothing about its inner workings. But there wasn't any need for me to know, for it was my job to coordinate and carry out the coming and going of equipment in need of repair. I therefore often found myself on "business trips" to the units, which had by then moved closer together as the partisan-free areas were constantly growing smaller. I picked up sets and brought new ones with me, so that an on-the-spot exchange could take place. It was actually a comfortable position, even though I had to pass through areas threatened by partisans now and then.

One day I was present when British aircraft dropped supply containers. Someone said to me, "Come on! Come with us, we're going to get them." And in fact a growing percentage of our equipment and armament was of British origin. Their submachine-guns in particular were coveted. As the comrade had said it so matter-of-factly, I went with him and about ten of us walked to the drop site. As we approached, we saw that a large number of civilians—they were not partisans—were at the drop site and were opening the supply containers. Shouts of "Piss off out of here!" and grim-looking German soldiers soon caused the people to scamper away. We couldn't hang around for long either, as the partisans would soon be coming. So we hurried over to see what was there. Dressings, first-aid equipment with instructions—in English of course—but also sweets, and they were most welcome. Then it was time to get out of there.

Thank God I had no more extreme situations. All went well. On April 16, 1945, my new post moved to Porpetto (approximately nine miles south of Udine) on the Adriatic coast. The *II. Bataillon* of our *Waffen-Gebirgs[Karstjäger]-Regiment der SS 59* was stationed there to secure the area inland of the coast. I was issued new collar patches with embroidered silver thistles instead of SS runes. Probably everyone in the *II. Bataillon* received these collar patches, including the German core personnel, but I cannot recall seeing anyone who had sewn the things on. There was an order to do so, but no one followed it. We also saw this as a disparagement, for we were proper SS members and not Italians or Slovenians who had been forcibly drafted.

Barely two weeks later, on April 29, 1945, we left the place and at about 2200—on account of Allied air superiority—marched off in the direction of Gonars. We arrived there in the early morning hours of April 30. The next night we proceeded via Udine to Tricesimo. From there we marched through Gemona and Venzone to Moggio Udine, arriving there on May 3, 1945. It was there that we learned of the surrender of the German troops in Italy.

On May 6, 1945, we left Moggio at about 1100—with the war over there was no danger of being attacked from the air—and at about 1400 crossed the Italian border. Members of the radio repair section and I spent the night at a military police post and then on the afternoon of May 7, 1945, we arrived in the Feistritz–Nötsch–Tröpolach area. Things were very well organized and at seven the next morning we left by bus for Spittal and Salzburg. We spent the

The collar patch bearing the karst thistle was issued to members of *II. Waffen-Gebirgs[Karstjäger]-Regiment der SS 59* in the spring of 1944.

The *Edelweiss* emblem for mountain troops.

The *Edelweiss* emblem was worn on the left sleeve of the field blouse and coat.

This insignia was worn on the left side flap of the mountain cap.

night outside Radstadt and on May 9, were transported by truck to Zell am See.

The unconditional surrender of the German armed forces was announced. There was no outbreak of joy from any of us. We had been spared the horrors of the Eastern Front or the invasion front, we had been relatively well supplied, and if one ignores the absence of fuel for our vehicles, we had been an intact and combat-ready unit until the end.

At about eight o'clock on Ascension Day we reached Salzburg and at 1400, we marched into one of the first reception camps for German prisoners of war. We spent three weeks in this camp, which with about 28,000 soldiers was completely overcrowded and unable to meet even the most primitive requirements. Then, in pouring rain, trucks took us to Kronau, which was about seventy miles to the northeast as the crow flies. We spent the night there in barns. From June 1–15, 1945, we were in barns near isolated Witting (approximately five miles southwest of Grafing near Munich). As we assumed that we would soon be released, no one ran away.

We then spent just under eighteen weeks in the Hohenfels prisoner of war camp. In front of the gate to the camp, which had probably been part of Training Camp Hohenfels, an American soldier sat at a table and collected our watches. Why, I do not know. It must have been an official order "from above." In any cases our watches were gone and ended up in a huge pile of wrist and pocket watches. None of us ever saw them again. The camp commander was an American who didn't care too much about the approximately 5,000 German prisoners of war. We lay on straw and each had just a wool blanket to cover himself.

From October 26, 1945 to February 19, 1946, I was in the SS prisoner of war camp at Plattling. The prisoners of war were initially housed in tents there—three men used their or available triangular tent sections to make a tent. Then barracks were set up. They were called blocks, as had been the case in the concentration camps. The prisoners of war built ten large barracks using wooden beams and boards, each one fenced in. The Americans called them cages. A wide road led through the Plattling camp, with five fenced-in cages on each side. Up to 1,000 members of the SS were penned up in each cage. If I recall correctly, the German camp commander was an *SS-Obersturmbannführer* Cäsar, his deputy was *SS-Obersturmbannführer* Neumann. We received very little to eat, and we gathered up cigarette butts discarded by the Amis. Some of our guards were Americans, but there were also Poles and Germans who had probably been in concentration camps. Treatment varied. The Poles abused and kicked us without end, and the former concentration camp inmates mocked us: "You could never have dreamed that one day you would be guarded by us, you members of the master race!" In addition to us Germans, Russian, and Ukrainian SS volunteers were also housed at Plattling. I recall the beautiful melancholy Russian songs sung in a deep bass. Christmas 1945 was very nice. There were many Christmas trees in front of and inside the barracks and … we were finally able to write home! The Amis gave us special writing paper. One wrote with pen and water (sic!), for the paper turned blue wherever it was wet. Evacuation of the camp began in mid-January 1946. Many were taken by truck in a hair-raising drive to Dachau. Rumors circulated that they were going to move refugees into the camp.

Four weeks later it was my turn, and I was transferred to Auerbach, an American prisoner of war camp at Training Camp Grafenwöhr. Actually it was Bernreuth, the former western camp of the big German training camp, which is still there. The Americans renamed the camp "Prisoner of War Enclosure Auerbach" (POW Camp 24). The barracks camp initially had no fence. The German prisoners of war had to make one and place a watchtower every fifty meters. The camp was lit bright as day all night long. The inmates must have given the Amis the jitters. Initially about 3,500 female flak auxiliaries and signals auxiliaries were housed there. Then came *Wehrmacht* prisoners of war and finally members of the SS, including author Günter Grass. The camp turned into an almost exclusive SS camp and with more than 10,000 SS members was one of the largest in Germany.* When I was there they were already using Poles as guards and they often behaved like bulls in a china shop. I remember one time when several Poles, falling down drunk, fired at random into the camp, killing several comrades. Good Friday 1946—it was April 19—a poison attack was made against us. Jews, who probably worked in a bakery or had access to it, laced bread dough with arsenic. We were among those who received this bread and many of us developed symptoms of poisoning. Many lost their sight, others their teeth. I was lucky and probably received little or no arsenic in my bread ration.

Whether it was a result of the poison attack or not, the Americans began releasing prisoners in large numbers. The camp emptied quickly and my turn came on Wednesday, May 29, 1946. I was released and took the train back to my former life. The Auerbach camp was closed soon afterward.

My parents were happy that I was home again just a year after the war. Oh the suffering of other families, some of whom had to wait for their sons and husbands until 1955, or who waited in vain because their family members died in captivity. I found a job immediately and then in 1958 I moved to the German Employees

*In 1946 the largest SS Prisoner of War and Internment Camps were:

Altenstadt	2,037 inmates	Auerbach	10,488 inmates
Babenhausen	17,140 inmates	Bad Aibling	7,637 inmates
Dachau	20,687 inmates	Flossenbürg	4,596 inmates
Göggingen	1,965 inmates	Hallein	4,325 inmates
Ingostadt	3,097 inmates	Memmingen	1,239 inmates
Nuremberg-Langwasser	11,761 inmates	Plattling	2,786 inmates
Regensburg	11,049 inmates	Ziegenhain	4,973 inmates

Health Insurance. I worked there for thirty years until I retired.

As well as my family and career, music was compensation for me. I joined a music society and I was even on its board from 1952–54, and again from 1956–61. I also got a great deal of enjoyment from nature. Together with my wife, I became a field ornithologist and learned to identify birds both by their plumage and song. We led bird song hikes and often began them at five or six in the morning. Behind our house alone, over the years we observed and identified forty-two species of bird. Sadly all that is in the past, as I fell ill with Parkinson's disease in 1990.

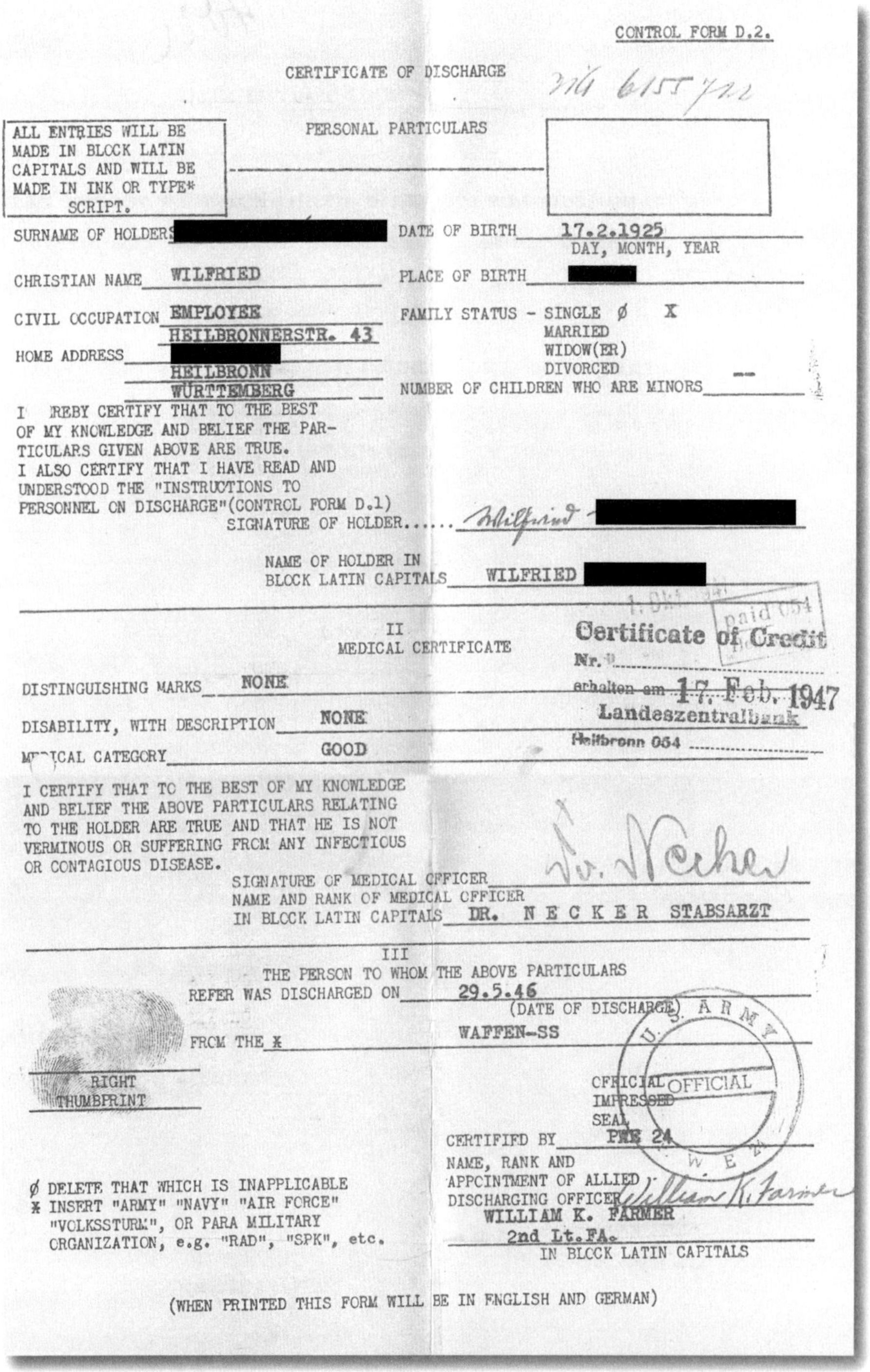

CONTROL FORM D.2.

CERTIFICATE OF DISCHARGE

MG 6155722

ALL ENTRIES WILL BE MADE IN BLOCK LATIN CAPITALS AND WILL BE MADE IN INK OR TYPE* SCRIPT.

PERSONAL PARTICULARS

SURNAME OF HOLDER [redacted] DATE OF BIRTH 17.2.1925
DAY, MONTH, YEAR

CHRISTIAN NAME WILFRIED PLACE OF BIRTH [redacted]

CIVIL OCCUPATION EMPLOYEE FAMILY STATUS - SINGLE Ø X
MARRIED
WIDOW(ER)
DIVORCED

HOME ADDRESS HEILBRONNERSTR. 43
HEILBRONN
WÜRTTEMBERG

NUMBER OF CHILDREN WHO ARE MINORS —

I HEREBY CERTIFY THAT TO THE BEST OF MY KNOWLEDGE AND BELIEF THE PARTICULARS GIVEN ABOVE ARE TRUE.
I ALSO CERTIFY THAT I HAVE READ AND UNDERSTOOD THE "INSTRUCTIONS TO PERSONNEL ON DISCHARGE" (CONTROL FORM D.1)

SIGNATURE OF HOLDER...... Wilfried [redacted]

NAME OF HOLDER IN BLOCK LATIN CAPITALS WILFRIED [redacted]

II
MEDICAL CERTIFICATE

Certificate of Credit
Nr. ...
erhalten am 17. Feb. 1947
Landeszentralbank
Heilbronn 054

DISTINGUISHING MARKS NONE

DISABILITY, WITH DESCRIPTION NONE

MEDICAL CATEGORY GOOD

I CERTIFY THAT TO THE BEST OF MY KNOWLEDGE AND BELIEF THE ABOVE PARTICULARS RELATING TO THE HOLDER ARE TRUE AND THAT HE IS NOT VERMINOUS OR SUFFERING FROM ANY INFECTIOUS OR CONTAGIOUS DISEASE.

SIGNATURE OF MEDICAL OFFICER Dr. Necker

NAME AND RANK OF MEDICAL OFFICER IN BLOCK LATIN CAPITALS DR. N E C K E R STABSARZT

III
THE PERSON TO WHOM THE ABOVE PARTICULARS REFER WAS DISCHARGED ON 29.5.46
(DATE OF DISCHARGE)

FROM THE * WAFFEN-SS

RIGHT THUMBPRINT

OFFICIAL IMPRESSED SEAL
U.S. ARMY OFFICIAL

CERTIFIED BY PWE 24

NAME, RANK AND APPOINTMENT OF ALLIED DISCHARGING OFFICER William K. Farmer
WILLIAM K. FARMER
2nd Lt. FA.
IN BLOCK LATIN CAPITALS

Ø DELETE THAT WHICH IS INAPPLICABLE
* INSERT "ARMY" "NAVY" "AIR FORCE" "VOLKSSTURM", OR PARA MILITARY ORGANIZATION, e.g. "RAD", "SPK", etc.

(WHEN PRINTED THIS FORM WILL BE IN ENGLISH AND GERMAN)

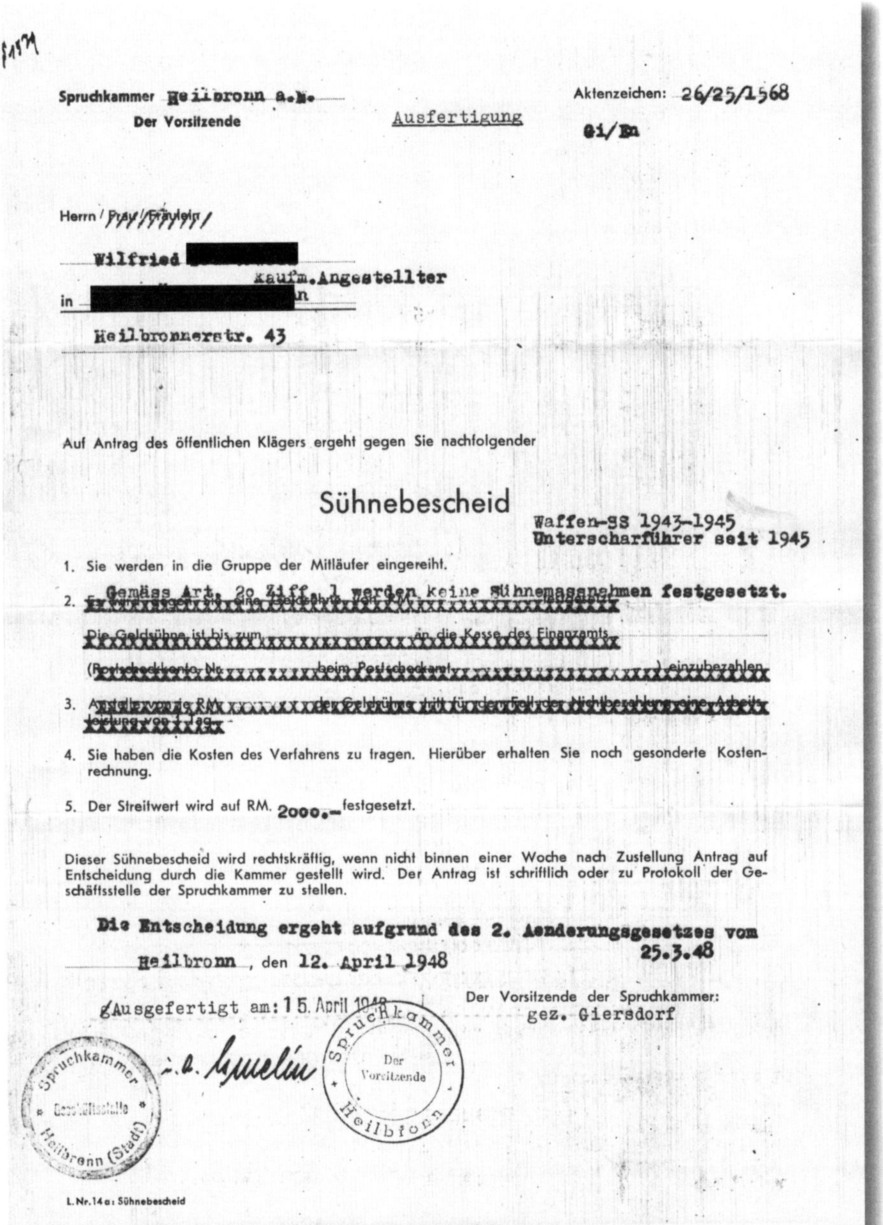

Spruchkammer Heilbronn a.N.
Der Vorsitzende

Ausfertigung

Aktenzeichen: 26/25/1568
Gi/Em

Herrn / ~~Frau / Fräulein~~

Wilfried [redacted]
kaufm.Angestellter
in [redacted]

Heilbronnerstr. 43

Auf Antrag des öffentlichen Klägers ergeht gegen Sie nachfolgender

Sühnebescheid

Waffen-SS 1943-1945
Unterscharführer seit 1945

1. Sie werden in die Gruppe der Mitläufer eingereiht.
2. Gemäss Art. 20 Ziff. 1 werden keine Sühnemassnahmen festgesetzt.
3. ~~Anstelle von je RM. ... der Geldsühne tritt für den Fall der Nichtbezahlung eine Arbeitsleistung von 1 Tag.~~
4. Sie haben die Kosten des Verfahrens zu tragen. Hierüber erhalten Sie noch gesonderte Kostenrechnung.
5. Der Streitwert wird auf RM. 2000.- festgesetzt.

Dieser Sühnebescheid wird rechtskräftig, wenn nicht binnen einer Woche nach Zustellung Antrag auf Entscheidung durch die Kammer gestellt wird. Der Antrag ist schriftlich oder zu Protokoll der Geschäftsstelle der Spruchkammer zu stellen.

Die Entscheidung ergeht aufgrund des 2. Aenderungsgesetzes vom 25.3.48

Heilbronn, den 12. April 1948

Der Vorsitzende der Spruchkammer:
gez. Giersdorf

Ausgefertigt am: 15. April 1948

i.A. Gmelin

L.Nr.14a: Sühnebescheid

The document which designated Wilfried Sonnenthal as a "*Mitläufer*" in 1948. The term, used in denazification hearings in Germany, referred to people who were not charged with Nazi crimes but whose involvement with the Nazis was considered significant to an extent that they could not be exonerated for the crimes of the Nazi regime.

Appendix 1: The History of the *24. Waffen-Gebirgs[Karstjäger]-Division der SS*

The Origins of the *SS-Karstwehr*

Interestingly, the roots of the later *24. Waffen-Gebirgs[Karstjäger]-Division der SS* can be found in the civilian world. The Study Society for Primordial Intellectual History, German Ancestral Heritage was founded in Berlin on January 1, 1935. Its initiators were the *Reichsführer-SS* Heinrich Himmler and Dr. Herman Wirth, originally from the Netherlands. In the 1920s, Wirth had established a collection for "Folkloristic Customs and Ancient Religions" and in 1932, founded the Institute for Intellectual Prehistory in Bad Doberan.

Wirth believed that in the Neolithic Period the Germanic peoples had lived peacefully in a matriarchal social order and aspired to a return to this "primitive state." Himmler, who was chairman of the study society, was very interested in Wirth's research, however he rejected the idea of a matriarchy. As there was no agreement, in 1938, Dr. Wirth lost his position in the study society, which on January 1, 1939, was renamed the Research and Teaching Community of Ancestral Heritage (*Das Ahenerbe*). Its foremost task now was to research the "scope, spirit, deeds and heritage of the northern Indo-European races." In April 1940, the Research and Teaching Community was incorporated into the personal staff of the *Reichsführer-SS*.

Already in July 1937, Himmler directed the study society to systematically inventory and investigate the caves in Germany. This was intended to secure archaeological evidence for historical research. Two months after Austria was incorporated into the German Reich in March 1938, a karst and cave research center in Salzburg. In March 1939, this research institute was moved to Munich. Head of the institute, which concerned itself with general karst and cave research, karst geology, prehistoric speleology with particular focus on anthropology, zoology and botany, and the defense applications of speleology, was cave researcher Dr. Hans Brand.

In the course of military exploitation of civilian research facilities, in July 1942, the Institute for Military Science Applied Research was set up within the Research and Teaching Community of Ancestral Heritage. Among its tasks were:

- biological warfare and disease research
- defense medicine research
- applied mathematics and plant genetics, and
- defense geology important to the war effort.

For the latter field, the karst and cave research facilities were attached to the new institute. Research objectives were simultaneously modified and adapted to suit the war. Among other things, the members were now to determine to what extent caves and other underground spaces could be used as bomb-proof production sites for the armaments industry.

The *SS-Karstwehr-Kompanie*

When, on March 1, 1942, orders were issued for the creation of an SS volunteer mountain division in Serbia from ethnic Germans in southeastern Europe, the head of the karst and cave research institute, Dr. Brand, suggested to the *Reichsführer-SS* that he make military use of the institute's knowledge.

As this mountain division's future area of operations against the partisans would be a karst region with its geological peculiarities,

Dr. Brand planned courses to teach the officers and non-commissioned officers all militarily useful information about karst formations and caves.

Himmler took up the proposal and on July 3, 1942, ordered the formation of an *SS-Karstwehr-Kompanie* at the SS camp at Dachau. Company personnel was to consist of one officer, eight non-commissioned officers and sixty-five enlisted men. Dr. Brand, the sixty-three-year-old head of the Karst and Cave Research Facility, was named company commander.

The company was originally organized into a:

- Karst training squad
- Karst pioneer platoon and
- *Karstjäger* (light infantry) platoon.

As early as September 1942, high-mountain karst courses were prepared near Alt-Aussee in the Totengebirge, a group of mountains in Austria, part of the Northern Limestone Alps. Barracks camps near Werfen-Wenig in the Tennen Mountains and the Birgkarhaus on the Hochkönig were ultimately used. In addition to the high-mountain courses, low mountain range karst courses were to be held in Pottenstein (Central Franconia), with the former hospital initially serving as quarters. Preparations for construction of a permanent training ground finally began at the end of September 1942.

In October 1942, the members of *SS-Sonderkommando "K"* also began mountain training. After the conquest of the Caucasian oil fields near Maykop, Himmler had ordered the Research and Teaching Community of Ancestral Heritage to research the Caucasus. A scientific expedition headed by *SS-Sturmbannführer* Dr. Ernst Schäfer was supposed to carry out entomological, geophysical, and anthropological investigations of the entire Caucasus.

By order of the *SS-Führungshauptamt*, *SS-Sonderkommando "K"* was to be formed at the SS barracks in Dachau effective September 15, 1942. In addition to the members of the Research and Teaching Community of Ancestral Heritage, members of the *Waffen-SS* were detached to escort the scientists and trained at Pottenstein until mid-December 1942. Negative developments on the Eastern Front resulted in the expedition being cancelled, however.

With the 6th Army facing destruction at Stalingrad, *SS-Sonderkommando "K"* was disbanded effective January 29, 1943. The secondment of the assigned members of the *Waffen-SS* ended on February 4, 1943. The majority were taken over by the new *SS-Karstwehr-Bataillon*. The Research and Teaching Community of Ancestral Heritage reserved the plans for the expedition until January 1944, when they were then also set aside.

Excursus: it cannot be assumed that the *SS-Karstwehr-Kompanie* was also supposed to take part in "Operation Hercules," the occupation of Malta, but this circulates among the former members. Action on Malta would have been theoretically possible, as the island also had many karst ranges of hills. The unit's very specialized training would thus have been useful there. On May 4, 1942, Hitler ordered "Operation Hercules" to go ahead in July 1942. At that time the *SS-Karstwehr-Kompanie* had just received its formation order, so participation would not have been possible at that time.

The more than 1,000 aircraft required for the invasion of Malta were not released because of the heavy fighting in North Africa. The occupation of Malta was postponed until a later date. In autumn 1942 the *SS-Karstwehr-Kompanie* was enlarged into a battalion and explicitly attached to the SS General Command (Panzer), thus excluding any hypothetical use on Malta. Army Group Africa surrendered soon afterwards, making the occupation of the island irrelevant.

The *SS-Karstwehr-Bataillon*

Formation

After the *SS-Führungshauptamt* ordered the formation of an SS Corps Headquarters for a corps at Training Camp Bergen–Fallingbostel on June 1, 1942, in July 1942, it ordered it transferred to the 15th Army in northern France and finally to the southern France in the Avillon area. There the attached units were reorganized and prepared for use in the Caucasus. As there were numerous karst regions there, on November 19, 1942, orders were issued for the existing *SS-Karstwehr-Kompanie* to be expanded into a battalion and attached to the newly-created SS Corps Headquarters (Panzer). As the formation order contained the explicit wording *"for the SS Corps Headquarters (Panzer),"* it was obvious that the unit would no longer be used as a training body, but instead would be attached to the corps headquarters as a corps unit for active use in the field.

On November 30, 1942, the new battalion's strength stood at four officers, twenty-six non-commissioned officers, and 172 enlisted men. Not until February 1943, was its personnel strength increased, when the roughly 100 members of the disbanded *SS-Sonderkommando "K"* joined the battalion. About 200 members of the *SS-Gebirgsjäger-Ersatz-Bataillon "Nord"* (SS Mountain Infantry Replacement Battalion "North") from Trautenau followed in March 1943, and on April 30, 1943 the *SS-Karstwehr-Bataillon* was organized as follows:

Headquarters:	3 officers	6 NCOs	1 enlisted man
HQ Company:	1 officer	27 NCOs	161 enlisted men
1st Company:	2 officers	9 NCOs	205 enlisted men
4th Company:	1 officer	5 NCOs	195 enlisted men

The battalion thus had a total strength of seven officers, forty-seven non-commissioned officers, and 562 enlisted men. In January 1943, in response to the Soviet winter offensive, the SS Corps Headquarters

(Panzer) was hastily ordered into the Kharkov area. As the battalion was not yet operational, it was not sent with the corps headquarters, remaining instead in Pottenstein. Himmler subsequently changed plans and ordered that, once its formation was complete, the *SS-Karstwehr-Bataillon* was to be transferred to Slovenia, to the area around the 9,393-foot Triglav. In the Julian Alps it was to be attached to the Senior SS and Police Commander "Alpenland," *SS-Gruppenführer* Roesener and be employed against Slovenian partisans.

Initially, however, the formation process went on. Not until June 1943 could the 2nd Company be formed from members of the *SS-Panzergrenadier-Schule* (SS Panzer Grenadier School) in Posen-Treskau and the 3rd Company using ethnic Germans from Rumania, who had already been drafted to serve in *SS-Grenadier-Ersatz-Bataillon "Ost"* (SS Grenadier Replacement Battalion "East").

When, effective July 1, 1943, the corps headquarters of the *V. SS-Gebirgs-Korps* (V SS Mountain Corps) was formed for use in the Balkans, the *SS-Karstwehr-Bataillon* was attached as a corps unit, as had once been envisaged for the SS Corps Headquarters (Panzer). Together with the *SS-Freiwilligen-Gebirgs-Division "Prinz Eugen"* (SS Volunteer Mountain Division "Prinz Eugen") and the *Kroatischen SS-Freiwilligen-Gebirgs-Division* (Croatian SS Volunteer Mountain Division), the battalion was to be used against the numerous partisan formations in the Croatian and Serbian karst regions. The battalion commander, *SS-Standartenführer* Brandt, took a skeptical view of this attachment. He wrote to Himmler that only a deployment for a limited time made sense, for, "if the intention of this transfer is a lasting integration into a mountain corps, then the further unhindered development of the *SS Karstjäger* force and the associated further expansion of the karst training installation in Pottenstein will be called into question."

After events developed rapidly, such desires could no longer be taken into consideration.

Into Combat 1943

The political upheaval in Italy, which saw Mussolini relieved of his offices on July 25, 1943, immediately triggered German countermeasures. These included fortification of the border crossings to Italy. In the course of these reactions the *SS-Karstwehr-Bataillon* was also placed on alert. It was transported by rail to *II. SS-Panzer-Korps* in the area around Villach. The formation was thus removed from *V. SS-Gebirgs-Korps*, which was then being formed. Attached to Battle Group Bredenförder of the *71. Infanterie-Division*, the battalion was now under the corps headquarters for which it had originally been planned in November 1942.

After the Italian High Command sent troops to reinforce the border fortifications and prepared strategic points for demolition, the reinforced *71. Infanterie-Division* received orders to proceed to Italy on August 26, 1943. For the *SS-Karstwehr-Bataillon* this meant crossing the border near Tarvis and marching into the Camporosso–Boscoverde area. There it was welcomed by the local ethnic Germans and assumed responsibility for guarding the rail line between Villach and Gemona.

The Italian High Command vigorously protested these moves by the Germans and declared that any further advance into Italy by German units would be prevented by force of arms. The break in the former alliance was thus just a matter of time. On August 30, 1943, Army Group B was issued new orders for Case Axis, the departure of Italy from the former alliance with Germany. When the codeword was issued, the army group was to take the following actions:

a) Reinforce all mountain crossings.
b) Occupy Genoa, La Spezia, and Livorno, as well as Trieste, Fiume, and Pola.
c) Secure the most important Appenine crossings between Genoa and Florence.
d) Pacify northern Italy.

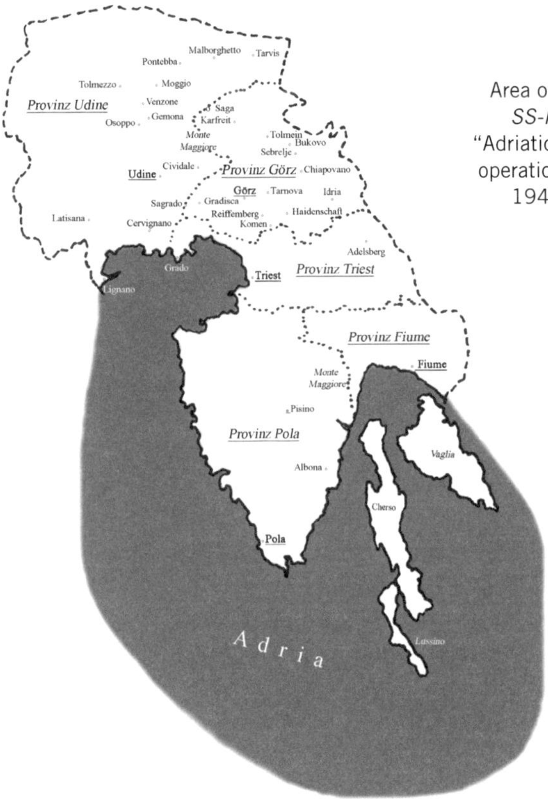

Area of operations of the *SS-Karstjäger* in the "Adriatic Coastland" zone of operations from September 1943 to May 1945.

On September 7, 1943, tensions between Germany and Italy reached such a level that Hitler planned to hand the Italian government an ultimatum. This contained numerous demands, and if these were not met Germany would take more extensive measures for the security and combat use of its forces in Italy. The note was unnecessary, for the next day the Italian ceasefire with the Allies was announced. "Operation Axis" began at 2000.

The *SS-Karstwehr-Bataillon* was subsequently employed to disarm Italian troops near Pontebba, Uggowitza, and Raibel on the night of September 8–9, 1943. As these followed the orders issued by Italian King Victor Emanuel III, and now looked on their former German allies as the enemy, there was fighting, in some places heavy.

On September 16, 1943, the commander of Battle Group *Bredenförder* (*Major* Bredenförder) composed a letter of recognition for the *SS-Karstwehr-Bataillon*, which was attached to his battle group:

> Following the betrayal by the Badoglio government, the German *Wehrmacht*, including Battle Group *Bredenförder*, received orders to disarm the Italian Army. In the sector of the *SS-Karstwehr-Bataillon*, which since entering Italy on August 26, 1943, had secured the important Villach – Gemona rail line in exemplary fashion, the battalion found itself facing numerically far superior Italian garrisons, which could fall back on large quantities of weapons, ammunition, clothing and food. Despite this, after negotiations with the commanders of the Italian troops failed to convince them to lay down their arms, the battalion attacked with great verve early on September 9, 1943, and took its assigned objectives, often in fierce close combat. At 1000, the battalion was able to report that the last resistance had been broken in Tarvisio. Sixteen brave SS non-commissioned officers and men had to pay for their enthusiasm with their lives. Fifty members of the *SS-Karstwehr-Bataillon* were wounded, some of them seriously. This first action by the battalion has demonstrated that its officers, NCOs, and enlisted men are determined and tough fighters. I know that I can wholeheartedly rely on the *SS-Karstwehr-Bataillon* at all times.

During an inspection of the *SS-Karstwehr-Bataillon* in mid-September 1943, the commanding general of the *II. SS-Panzer-Korps* (*SS-Obergruppenführer* Hausser) advised that the formation would remain in the Tarvisio area for the time being. After disarming the Italian soldiers, the unit secured the area against partisans. In the days that followed, the unit frequently saw action in the Karfreit–Flitscher Klause area.

October 3, 1943, saw the end of the battalion's attachment to Battle Group Bredenförder, which followed *71. Infanterie-Division* into the Pola area. The battalion was then attached to the "von le Fort" Security Group (elements of the *188. Reserve-Gebirgs-Division*).

The clearing of the two valleys of the Natisone and the upper Isonzo was designated *Wolkenbruch* (Cloudburst). During these actions, on October 11, 1943, the village of Strmc was burned down as a reprisal for partisan attacks in this area and sixteen men between the ages of fifteen and fifty were shot. Still attached to *II. SS-Panzer-Korps*, the battalion subsequently took part in "Operation Traufe" on November 15, 1943. To deceive the enemy, during the operation the corps was designated *1. SS-Panzer-Armee* (SS-Pz.A.O.K. 1).

Together with elements of *Gebirgsjäger-Ersatz- und Ausbildungs-Regiment 139* (Mountain Infantry Replacement and Training Regiment 139), the battalion moved into the area west of Laibach. Deployed against powerful partisan units in the area around Logatec–Idria–Skolfia Loka–Val Baccia (Baccia Valley), and other units, including *Polizei-Regiment 19*, also took part. After this operation concluded, on November 20, 1943, the German units pursued escaped partisans into the Sorica–Poce area in the Baccia Valley.

On November 22, 1943, the battalion received orders to move to the *V. SS-Freiwilligen-Gebirgs-Korps* (V SS Volunteer Mountain Corps). *SS-Standartenführer* Dr. Brand vehemently opposed this, as he feared that his formation would lose its original special status. After another of his many letters to the *Reichsführer-SS*, he succeeded in having the *SS-Karstwehr-Bataillon* remain in the area assigned to it in the spring of 1943.

Four days later the unit was attached to the Senior SS and Police Commander Adriatic Coastland under *SS-Gruppenführer und Generalleutnant der Polizei* Globocnik. On December 1, 1943, followed the transfer to the barracks in Gradisca d'Isonzo (approximtely nine miles southwest of Görz) and Sagrado, approximately thirty-five miles to the south.

By order of Himmler, in this area the battalion was to:

– clear the area of partisans,
– set up at least two fixed garrisons, and
– assist the Senior SS and Police Commander Adriatic Coastland in establishing
native formations.

In the second week of December, *Einsatzkompanie "Kühbandner"* (Operational Company Kühbander), with a strength of 212 men, was formed from elements of the Headquarters Company and the 2nd and 4th Companies. It took part in "Operation Blumendraht" (Florist's Wire) from December 12–14. Assembled in the area of Nimes (approximately nine miles north of Udine), roughly twenty-eight miles to the northwest, the soldiers marched through Cergneu to Nongruella as part of Battle Group "von le Fort." There were frequent battles with partisans.

At the end of December 1943, the *SS-Karstwehr-Bataillon* reported the following strength in its base at Gradisca:

Officers	**NCOs**	**Men**	**Total**
8	117	821	946
0.08%	12.4%	86.8%	100%

It was organized as follows:

Battalion Headquarters:	approx. 20 men
Headquarters Company:	approx. 160 men
1st *Jäger* Company:	approx. 170 men
2nd *Jäger* Company:	approx. 170 men
3rd *Jäger* Company:	approx. 170 men
4th (Heavy) Company:	approx. 170 men
Artillery Battery:	approx. 80 men

In September 1943, the *SS-Karstwehr-Bataillon* received additional equipment, including two Italian 75 mm guns. Like the 65 mm mountain cannon, with their wooden wheels they were not designed to be towed by motor vehicles. Despite this, in the photo above an Italian Fiat Spa TL 37 is seen towing a gun. Italian troops served in the artillery battalion until the end of the war.

In the Karst Mountains mules proved indispensible for transporting heavy weapons and equipment. Here mules are transporting a disassembled 65 mm mountain cannon.

The Artillery Battery had been equipped with captured Italian guns. While the battalion had a large number of enlisted men, it was far below strength in non-commissioned officers and officers. The shortfall in officers was particularly serious, with approximately 60% of the authorized positions unfilled.

Combat Operations 1944

Because of the missing officers, only parts of the battalion took part in "Operation Edelweiß," which was carried out on January 15, 1944, and these were again attached to Battle Group "von le Fort." Together with elements of the *188. Reserve-Gebirgs-Division*, the SS men were initially committed in the area south of the eighteen-mile-wide line from Görz to Haidenschaft (Aidussina). There was fighting in Lokve (approximately 4.5 miles northeast of Tarnova), Predmeia (approximately nine miles southeast of Tarnova), and Chiapovano (approximately nine miles northeast of Tarnova). The operation against Slovenian partisans ended after fourteen days. Partisan quarters and depots were discovered in Lokve and the village of thirty-two houses was subsequently burned and five residents shot. This was immediately followed by "Operation Enzian" (Gentian) in the area of Monte Santo (northeast of Görz), where there had been heavy fighting on the Isonzo front during the First World War.

As the *SS-Karstwehr-Bataillon* had been given the task of assisting the Senior SS and Police Commander Adriatic Coastland in forming domestic formations at the end of November 1943, on January 6, 1944, *SS-Standartenführer* Dr. Brand proposed to Hitler forming an SS karst defense unit from Slovenian volunteers:

> Training in Pottenstein will teach these people to come to know and appreciate German ways and also give them contact with German karst folk, who are in an equally hard struggle for existence, and thus more easily separate them from their former Bolshevik influences and ways of thinking. The

> Slovenian people, extremely hard-working, loyal and highly developable, raised very close to the land, who are especially dear to my heart, can then, with special state status, become an exemplary German protectorate under German leadership.

The situation in the Adriatic Coastland, however, was extraordinarily unfavorable for recruitment. The communist partisans—who formed the Liberation Front (Osvobodilna Fronta) in 1941—controlled large areas of the country. While the bulk of the population did not follow them politically, after their previous experiences they were opposed to German–Italian policies. Attempts to counter this situation included the formation of *Kommando Adria* within the *SS-Standarte "Kurt Eggers."* Small propaganda teams were supposed to attract natives to the German side. *SS-Unterscharführer* Fuhrmann, leader of *Einsatztruppe Görz*, described the situation as follows:

> To give our propaganda work broader impact, in various towns with *Wehrmacht* bases I interested these units in our work and set up propaganda bases. We then regularly delivered out materials to them. They accompanied us during operations, patrols and so on, and took us to areas we had never been able to drive to in our vehicles because of the partisan threat.

Because of *SS-Standartenführer* Dr. Brand's Slovenophile stance, the *SS-Karstwehr-Bataillon* also participated actively in the recruiting. As well, elements of the battalion were in action against partisans almost daily. This usually took the form of partisans being reported or combat between them and German units. The *SS-Karstjäger* responded in platoon strength for reconnaissance or company strength to lend assistance [to units under attack]. For example, on February 15–16, the SS men took part in "Operation Ratte" (Rat). *III./SS-Polizei-Regiment 15* (III Battalion, SS Police Regiment 15) and units of the Commander of Security Police were also deployed south of Haidenschaft in the Reifenberg–Komen area. After members of the police were ambushed, the latter village was burned and the population deported to Germany for labor purposes.

"Operation Alpenrose" (Alpine Rose) followed from February 18–21, 1944. Together with elements of the *188. Reserve-Gebirgs-Division*, the *SS-Karstjäger* were deployed in the area between Tolmein and Cividale, where they were supposed to engage two Slovenian partisan brigades with a combined strength of about 1,200 men. During the heavy fighting, elements of the *SS-Karstwehr-Bataillon* were encircled by partisans for a time. Sixteen members of the battalion were killed and thirty wounded.

From March 3–5, 1944, the battalion took part in "Operation Zypresse" (Cypress) in the Doberdo area (approximately 3.5 miles southeast of Gradisca). "Operation Märzveilchen" (Sweet Violet) followed on March 12, 1944, and it was followed by "Operation Hellblau" (Pale Blue) on March 18. All of these actions took place in the area of Komen (approximately eleven miles east of Monfalcone).

On March 23, 1944, *SS-Hauptsturmführer* Berschneider assumed command of the battalion. As *SS-Standartenführer* Dr. Brand believed that he had the most experience in karst topography and therefore also for operations against partisans, there were repeated disputes with the Senior SS and Police Commander Adriatic Coastland. Himmler subsequently relieved Dr. Brand of command of the battalion and was placed in charge of the newly-built cave research facility in the Karst. In one of his countless letters to *SS-Sturmbannführer* Grothmann, Himmler's chief adjutant in his personal staff, Dr. Brand gave free rein to his displeasure:

> After a good initial relationship with the Senior SS and Police Commander, ever greater differences of opinion developed with regard to my necessary freedom of action and the tactically-correct employment of my unit. My military experience, amassed over forty-five years, and my almost

> forty years of intimate knowledge of the karst and its political conditions made no difference to him.
>
> Contrary to the views of the *Reichsführer-SS*, who sent me there for the aforementioned tasks, the specialist knowledge of the karst was glossed over. My SS karst special unit, which with its specialized companies first achieved the smallest operational unit in the battalion, was torn apart and over the head of its commander was given to the Wehrmacht in small battle groups or was committed at discretion. If all went well everything was fine, but if there was a failure, then it was because the unit lacked quality, for which the commander was held responsible. If the commander objects to these methods of operation, which must soon lead to the complete wearing down of this valuable special unit, then he is considered bothersome or too old and then, using every possible argument, the attacks begin.

The letter shows that Dr. Brand misunderstood the true situation. In a war in which only pragmatic decisions could be made because of great material and personnel inferiority, there was no place for such animosities.

Dr. Brand and Globocnik were not the only ones with differences of opinion about the fundamental power of command and responsibility for combating partisans. Himmler and *Generalfeldmarschall* Kesselring, the Commander-in-Chief Southwest, also had differing views on the subject. To clarify the situation, the *Wehrmacht* High Command decreed that overall responsibility for combating partisans in Italy was the responsibility of the Commander-in-Chief Southwest. However, as *SS-Obergruppenführer* Wolff, Supreme SS and Police Commander in Italy and his subordinate, took responsibility in the "Alpine Foreland" and "Adriatic Coastland" zones of operations, in practical terms command continued to be divided.

From March 25, 1944, elements of the *SS-Karstwehr-Bataillon* took part in "Operation Dachstein" (Roof Tile) as Group Berschneider.

Officers and non-commissioned officers of the *SS-Karstwehr-Bataillon* at the end of March 1944. Seated, from left to right: *SS-Obersturmführer* Kühgandner, *SS-Obersturmführer* Weiland, *Hauptmann* Bischetsrieder, *SS-Standartenführer* Dr. Brand, *SS-Hauptsturmführer* Berschneider, *SS-Hauptsturmführer* Ullm, and *SS-Untersturmführer* Vogel.

Officers of the *SS-Karstwehr-Bataillon* during a German–Italian soccer game in Gradisca.

Together with units of the *188. Reserve-Gebirgs-Division* and *SS-Polizei-Regimenter 15* and *19*, the battalion's men marched into the Tarnova forest (Zola–Adalsberg area). As was so often the case, no decisive success was achieved against the Slovenian partisans.

The large-scale "Operation Osterglocke" (Daffodil) began on March 31, 1944, and was to last two weeks. It was the first action in Istria. The German command feared an invasion of the peninsula by the western Allies, therefore the rear was to be permanently cleared of partisans. Group Berschneider, together with *Wehrmacht* and police units, combed the Pisino (German Mitterburg, approximately twenty-eight miles south of Trieste) area as far as Albona (approximately eighteen miles southeast of Pisino). Combating the partisans took on special importance as Tito wanted to bring the area under his influence from Croatia.

In addition to the company of the *SS-Karstwehr-Bataillon* deployed there, others were committed with the *SS-Gebirgsjäger-Ausbildungs- und Ersatz-Bataillon 7* to secure the Laibach–Trieste line. For Hitler's birthday, April 20, 1944, the *SS-Karstwehr-Bataillon* was ordered to Trieste, where it took part in a parade before *SS-Gruppenführer und Generalleutnant der Polizei* Globocnik, Senior SS and Police Commander "Adriatic Coastland."

Another action in Istria, dubbed "Braunschweig" (Brunswick), followed from April 26 to May 6, 1944. Together with elements of the *278. Infanterie-Division*, the *181. Reserve-Gebirgs-Division,* and several companies from *SS-Polizei-Regimenter 15* and *"Bozen,"* the *SS-Karstwehr-Bataillon* was committed in the area of Monte Maggiore (Croatian Učka)–Pivka Valley (German Sankt Peter, approximately thirty miles east of Trieste) –Brkini Mountains–Tschitschen Boden. At the cost of relatively light German casualties, about 1,800 (suspected) partisans were taken prisoner and 390 were "*destroyed*" in combat.

Following this action the *SS-Karstjäger* returned to Gradisca, about fifty-five miles away. There *SS-Standartenführer* Dr. Brand, the former commanding officer, was given a farewell with military honors by Gauleiter Rainer and *SS-Gruppenführer* Globocnik. *SS-Hauptsturmführer* Berschneider, who had already been leading the battalion in an acting capacity, became the new battalion commander.

From May 22–27, 1944, the SS-*Karstjäger* took part in "Operations Liane I–III" in the area Peternel–Casteldobra (approximately twelve miles north of Gradisca). This was followed on May 28–29, by "Operation Spitz" near Reifenberg (about twenty-two miles east of Gradisca). This was an action under the command of *SS-Obersturmführer* Kühbandner, who personally led the combined 2nd and 4th Companies. Kühbandner's nickname was "Spitz" as he had a dog of that breed.

The large-scale "Operation Annemarie" began on June 5, 1944. From Baccia Valley (German Batsch, approximately thirteen miles southeast of St. Peter), the *SS-Karstwehr-Bataillon* marched through Görz, where an Italian gas shell dump was also guarded temporarily, and Haidenschaft into the Trieste area. The battalion, with elements of *SS-Polizei-Regiment* ten, captured thirty-nine partisans. Another 108 were killed in battle. German casualties were three killed and twenty-three wounded. As just one Italian 105 mm artillery piece with sixty rounds of ammunition, a light machine-gun and one submachine-gun were captured, the question rises whether the 108 people killed in combat were in fact partisans. During this action, on June 11, 1944, *Reserve-Gebirgsjger-Regiment 139* handed several captured partisans over to the battalion, and two of these were beheaded in Indrijske Krnice (approximately 8.5 miles east of Chiapovano). The commander of *Reserve-Gebirgsjger-Regiment 139* obviously did not want to be held accountable for the killings.

On March 23, 1944, Himmler placed *SS-Standartenführer* Dr. Brand in command of the newly-created cave research facility in the karst region following differences of opinion with *SS-Gruppenführer* Globocnik, Senior SS and Police Commander "Adriatic Coastland." This photo was taken during his official farewell in Gradisca d'Isonzo.

Above from left to right: Friedrich Rainer, the Supreme Commissioner for the "Adriatic Coastland" Zone of Operations, *SS-Standartenführer* Dr. Brand, and the Senior SS and Police Commander Adriatic Coastland, *SS-Gruppenführer* Odilo Globocnik.

Dr. Brand proved unable to win with his ideas against *SS-Gruppenführer* Globocnik.

The *24. Waffen-Gebirgs [Karstjäger]-Division der SS*

Formation

Although compulsory military service was introduced in the Adriatic Coastland zone of operations in autumn 1943, out of fear of strikes and uprisings the mustering of age classes 1923 to 1925 did not take place until March 1944. Age classes 1914 to 1922, and 1926 were called up in June 1944. From these "*members of the Adriatic Coastland*" Himmler planned to form a *Waffen-Gebirgs[Karstjäger]-Division der SS* effective July 18, 1944. The designation *Waffen-Division der SS* was given to indicate that the new inductees did not meet the racial requirements of the *Waffen-SS*. The formulation that they were "*members of the Adriatic Coastland*" was because, from an ethnic point of view there was no homogenous nationality, instead consisting of at least Italians, Slovenians, and Croats.

The approximately 1,000-man-strong *SS-Karstwehr-Bataillon* was to form the foundation of the division. Leader of the activation staff was the former commander of *SS-Gebirgsjäger-Ausbildungs- und Ersatz-Bataillon 6* in Hallein, *SS-Sturmbannführer* Hahn, who was supposed to activate a unit with the following organization:

Division Headquarters,
Waffen-Gebirgs[Karstjäger]-Regiment der SS 59 (I – III Battalions)
Waffen-Gebirgs[Karstjäger]-Regiment der SS 60 (I – III Battalions)
Waffen-Gebirgs-Artillerie-Regiment der SS 24 (I – III Battalions)
SS-Gebirgs-Aufklärungs-Abteilung 24 (Mountain Reconnaissance Battalion)
SS-Gebirgs-Panzerjäger-Abteilung 24 (Mountain Anti-tank Battalion)
SS-Gebirgs-Pionier-Bataillon 24 (Mountain Engineer Battalion)

SS-Gebirgs-Feldersatz-Bataillon 24 (Mountain Replacement Training Battalion)
SS-Gebirgs-Sanitäts-Abteilung 24 (Mountain Medical Battalion)
SS-Gebirgs-Veterinär-Kompanie 24 (Mountain Veterinary Company)
SS-Gebirgs-Nachrichten-Abteilung 24 (Mountain Signals Battalion)
SS-Gebirgs-Ersatz-Kompanie 24 (Mountain Replacement Company)
Kdr. der SS-Div.-Nachschubtruppen 24 (Commander SS Division Supply Troops 24)
SS-Feldpostamt 24 (SS Field Post Office 24)
SS-Wirtschafts-Bataillon 24 (SS Economic Battalion)

The *SS-Führungshauptamt*'s plans could not be realized, however. Although one age class in the area of the Adriatic Coastland comprised at least 10,000 men, because of the existing conditions no significant drafting could be undertaken. In total, thirteen age classes were supposed to be drafted in the Adriatic Coastland by the summer of 1944. As the attitude of the population ranged from negative to hostile, the German side was forced to cease recruiting. The efforts to date had only attracted about 400 men to serve in the new division.

When it became apparent that not enough personnel would be coming from the Adriatic Coastland in the short term, about 500 South Tyroleans were sent to the new division from the Uggowitza and Malborghetto training camps. These men had been drafted into the *Ordnungspolizei* at Sterzing and Schlanders in the Alpine Foreland zone of operations in April and May 1944 and now were transferred to the *Waffen-SS*. Although the new units were supposed to be formed in the Aupa–Pontebba–Malborghetto–Moggio Udinese area bordering the German Reich, the new division's activation staff remained at the former location of the *SS-Karstwehr-Bataillon*'s headquarters in Gradisca. The same was true of the various platoons and companies, which remained in their garrisons, while others were ordered to the area around Tolmezzo for activation of the new division.

As stated earlier, lack of personnel meant that only a few units could be formed:

Activation Staff		Military Postal Number 40 731
Signals Platoon		Military Postal Number 34 445
Cavalry Platoon		
Engineer Platoon		Military Postal Number 28 007
Waffen-Gebirgs[Karstjäger]-Rgt. Der SS 1		Military Postal Number 57 542
	Headquarters Company	Military Postal Number 57 542 A
	Anti-tank Platoon	Military Postal Number 57 542 B
	Infantry Gun Platoon	Military Postal Number 57 542 C
I Battalion		Military Postal Number 05 219
	Headquarters Company	Military Postal Number 57 542
II Battalion		Military Postal Number 28 657
III Battalion		Military Postal Number 33 627
Waffen-Gebirgs[Karstjäger]-Artillerie-Rgt. Der SS		
Mountain Artillery Battery		Military Postal Number 22 224

1 panzer company		Military Postal Number 64 584
1 medical company		Military Postal Number 32 137
1 veterinary company		Military Postal Number 67 130
1 supply unit		Military Postal Number 26 760
1 replacement company		Military Postal Number 67 728
1 military post office		Military Postal Number 43 480

By September 20, 1944, in addition to the about 500 South Tyroleans and approximately 400 residents of the Adriatic Coastland, the unit was assigned an additional 100 ethnic and Reich Germans, resulting in the following strength figures:

	Officers	**NCOs**	**Enlisted Men**	**Total**
Actual	27	163	1,799	1,989
	1.4%	8.2%	90.4%	100%
Authorized	165	898	5,563	6,626
	2.4%	13.6%	84%	100%

The men from the Adriatic Coastland initially formed III Battalion. After it was shown that tanks could also play an important role in anti-partisan warfare, a panzer company was formed for the new *24. Waffen-Gebirgs[Karstjäger]-Division der SS* in Cividale (approximately twelve miles east of Udine). The company was issued a number of Italian Fiat P40 tanks. At the end of September 1944, the division, which was still under formation, had the following:

11 Italian P40 tanks
6 75-mm mountain guns
4 45-mm infantry guns
24 81.4-mm mortars
20 heavy machine-guns
75 light machine-guns
150 pistols
150 submachine-guns
1,250 rifles

Compared to its personnel strength, the unit obviously had too few weapons. At the same time the *SS-Karstwehr-Ersatz-Kompanie* (SS *Karstwehr* Replacement Company) was transferred from Pottenstein to Gradisca, initially for about four weeks, and then was also stationed in Cividale. Strength in the operational area was thus increased at least nominally.

Elements of the *SS-Karstwehr-Bataillon*—mainly of the 2nd Company—were organized into hunting detachments (*Jagdkommando*) during formation of the "division" and deployed in the area around Tolmezzo where partisans were very active. The first awards of the Anti-Partisan War Badge in Bronze and Silver, created in February 1944, to members of the *SS-Karstwehr-Bataillon* took place in Tolmezzo in September.

Larger actions began again after the reorganization of two or three battalions, after partisans proclaimed the *Zona Libera della Carnia e del Friuli* (Free Zone of Carnia and Friaul) in Ampezzo (approximately twelve miles west of Tolmezzo) on September 26, 1944. Until September 30, 1944, units of *Waffen-Gebirgs[Karstjäger]-Regiment der SS 1* (renamed *59* a short time later) also took part in "Operation Klagenfurt." The operation by units of the *Wehrmacht*, *Waffen-SS*, and *Ordnungspolizei* failed to achieve the desired success, however.

"Operation *Waldläufer*" (Ranger) followed in the same area from October 8–22, 1944. Elements of the *Waffen-Gebirgs[Karstjäger]-*

Regiment der SS 1 were committed with units of *SS-Polizei-Regimenter 10* and *15* and the *71. Infanterie-Division* between Tolmezzo and the border of the German Reich. Concerning these two operations, the following is from the application for the German Cross in Gold for *SS-Gruppenführer* Globocnik dated February 25, 1945:

> In "Operation *Klagenfurt*," the skillful disposition of his forces and response to the constantly-changing enemy situation resulted in the destruction of the partisans in this area. Serious crises were overcome through flexibility in deploying his troops and losses of 500 killed were ultimately inflicted on the enemy. 248 prisoners fell into German hands.
>
> During the second week of operations against the partisans, in addition to other operations, in particular he led "Operation *Waldläufer*" to a complete success. Although command faced the most difficult situations, here again the partisans were so hard hit that they were no longer able to field large units. With minimal casualties of our own, the enemy left 105 dead on the field, and 165 prisoners were brought in. Two German officers and seventy-one non-commissioned officers and men of the German police were freed from partisan captivity. The amount of booty taken was great.
>
> For the operations conducted by *Gruppenführer* Globocnik in the area of the province of Udine, which demanded unheard-of feats by leadership and the troops, in addition to a personal telex in the Honor Roll of the *Reichsführer-SS*, the *Reichsführer-SS* has announced: "The following have distinguished themselves through exceptional bravery and steadfastness in the month of October 1944: SS and police units under the command of *SS-Gruppenführer und Generalleutnant der Polizei* Globocnik in fighting with Tito groups east of Udine. I have personally expressed my acknowledgment to prominent units and individual fighters."

The *24. Waffen-Gebirgs[Karstjäger]-Division der SS* received further reinforcements in autumn 1944, about 300 more men from the Adriatic Coastland and roughly 170 Spanish volunteers. The latter were former members of the *250. (spanische) Infanterie-Division*, which had been formed to fight against the Soviet Union and was disbanded in 1943. On November 27, 1944 the Commander of the *Waffen-SS* Italy submitted a strength report for the *24. Waffen-Gebirgs[Karstjäger]-Division der SS*:

	Officers	**NCOs**	**Enlisted Men**	**Total**
Actual	42	258	2,179	2,479
	1.4%	8.2%	90.4%	100%
Authorized	165	898	5,563	6,626
	2.4%	13.6%	84%	100%

The following is an ethnic breakdown of the unit's personnel:

Reich Germans	750 men
Ethnic Germans	850 men
Inhabitants of the Adriatic Coastland	700 men
Spaniards	170 men

"Operation Axis" began on the same day that this report as compiled. Again under the command of *SS-Gruppenführer* Globocnik, the area of planned defense positions against the advancing British was to be cleared of partisans. Elements of the SS *Karstjäger* in Udine were also transferred to Tolmezzo for the operation. When the operation concluded on December 13, 1944, it was reported that 206 partisans had been killed, and 120 wounded.

"Operation Adler" (Eagle) followed in the Görz–Haidenschaft area from December 19–25. In preparation for the operation, the companies were again withdrawn from Tolmezzo and sent to the new area of operations. The following is from the previously-mentioned application for the German Cross in Gold for *SS-Gruppenführer* Globocnik:

> Operation *Adler* deprived the partisans of their entire supply base, drove them back into the inhospitable hills and also inflicted considerable losses upon them. The partisans lost 488 killed, 123 captured, and large quantities of war materiel.

The Division is Renamed the *Waffen-Gebirgs[Karstjäger]-Brigade der SS*

After it became apparent that the number of men recruited in the Adriatic Coastland was far too small to bring the *SS-Karstwehr-Bataillon* to division strength, on December 5, 1944, the unit was reduced to a *Waffen-Gebirgs[Karstjäger]-Brigade der SS*. The completed formation of the brigade by reclassifying the division was to be reported by January 30, 1945.

As no additional personnel were received, the unit's organization remained as before:

Activation Staff	*SS-Sturmbannführer* Hahn
Signals Platoon	*SS-Sturmscharführer* Ferensky
Cavalry Platoon	*Waffen-Obersturmführer* Borsatti
Engineer Platoon	*SS-Hauptscharführer* Trautmannsberg
Anti-tank Platoon	*SS-Oberscharführer* Stähle

Waffen-Gebirgs[Karstjäger]-Regiment der SS 59

I Battalion	*SS-Sturmbannführer* Berschneider
II Battalion	*SS-Obersturmführer* Merwald
III Battalion	*SS-Obersturmführer* Kühbandner

Waffen-Gebirgs[Karstjäger]-Artillerie-Regiment der SS 24

Mountain Artillery Battery	*SS-Untersturmführer* Wüst

SS-Karstjäger – above: *SS-Obersturmführer* Weiland in front of an Italian P40 tank knocked out by partisans.

SS-Obersturmführer Weiland, the battalion adjutant.

Panzer Company	*SS-Obersturmführer* Behrend
Medical Company	*SS-Hauptsturmführer* Dr. Habisreutinger
Supply Troops	*SS-Hauptsturmführer* Ulm
Replacement Company	*SS-Untersturmführer* Bender

It also proved impossible to complete the activation of the brigade by January 30, 1945. Instead there was increasing unreliability, especially among the Italian members, and soon orders were issued for *III./Waffen-Gebirgs[Karstjäger]-Regiment der SS 59* to disband.

Combat Operations 1945

In January 1945, *II./Waffen-Gebirgs[Karstjäger]-Regiment der SS 59* was transferred to the Grado–Lignano area, approximately fifty-five miles to the south. The South Tyrolean recruits had already taken part in a number of actions—for example standing guard over Cereschiatis Pass between Moggio Udinese and Pontebba—but the powers that be did not yet want to send them into direct anti-partisan operations. The area of Marano Lagoon was a potential landing site for the Allies and positions had to be built and manned there. The *Waffen-Gebirgs[Karstjäger]-Brigade der SS* was spread over an area about fifty-five miles long and thirty-five miles wide. I Battalion was in the Udine area and the Replacement Company and the Panzer Company in Gradisca. As III Battalion would not become operational, in spring 1945 it was disbanded in its quartering area in Tolmezzo and most of its core personnel were assigned to II Battalion. The Spanish volunteers formed the 5th Company. The 8th and 12th Companies were combined. Most of the remaining foreign volunteers were sent to the supply train to serve as pack animal leaders. The only unit which retained a certain number of Italians was the Mountain Artillery Battery.

In contrast to I Battalion, almost all of whose personnel were former members of the earlier *SS-Karstwehr-Bataillon*, in the spring of 1945, new collar patches were issued to II Battalion. Like all collar patches for the (foreign) *Waffen* units of the SS, they bore a single symbol. At the same time, on February 10, 1945, the brigade was renamed a division again to deceive the enemy. Although it received no additional personnel, its designation was again *24. Waffen-Gebirgs[Karstjäger]-Division der SS*.

From March 20, 1945, I Battalion took part in "Operation *Frühlingsanfang*" (First Day of Spring). Under the overall command of *SS-Standartenführer* Ludolf von Alvensleben, SS and Police Commander "Adriatic West" (formerly designated SS and Police Commander "Udine"), the operation, in which elements of the *1. SS-Kosaken-Kavallerie-Division* (1st SS Cossack Cavalry Division) also took part, ended on April 6, 1945. It took place in the area north of the Idrijca River in the Tarnov Forest.

Three days later the Allies opened their final offensive in Italy. On April 25, 1945, the British Eighth Army crossed the Po and advanced on Venice and Trieste. A hypothetical airborne landing was no longer a threat. On April 25, 1945, the Italian partisans called for a national uprising. Four days later the Allies reached Venice, which had been evacuated by German forces the day before. On April 29, 1945, the Supreme SS and Police Commander in Italy, *SS-Obergruppenführer und General der SS* Wolff, also signed the surrender of German troops in Italy in Caserta. As it required all German forces to immediately leave Italy, the retreat to the Reich border began.

When, at the end of April 1945, partisans blocked the road through the Tagliamento Road between Osoppo and Gemona, which was vital for the retreat, *I./Waffen-Gebirgs[Karstjäger]-Regiment der SS 59*, coming from the Udine area, was committed to reopen it. *II./Waffen-Gebirgs[Karstjäger]-Regiment der SS 59*, coming from the Adriatic coast, was attached to SS Battle Group Harmel. Its mission was to secure the greater Osoppo–Gemona–Venzone area. In addition to the SS *Karstjäger*, *SS-Brigadeführer* Harmel now also commanded *SS-Gebirgsjäger-Ausbildungs- und Ersatz Bataillon 7* and *SS-Polizei-Regiment 10*. SS Battle Group Harmel, about 5,000 men strong, was attached to *XXII. Gebirgs-Korps* (XXII Mountain Corps) under *General der Gebirgstruppen* Lanz. During the attempt to clear the area of the retreat, on May 2, 1945, fifty-one civilians were shot near Avasinis (approximately seven miles west of Gemona).

On April 29, 1945, on the Adriatic, *II./Waffen-Gebirgs[Karstjäger]-Regiment der* SS was alerted and initially assembled in San Giorgio de Nagaro. Moving only by night, from there it reached the positions in the Osoppo–Gemona area at the beginning of May 1945, relieving *I./Waffen-Gebirgs[Karstjäger]-Regiment der SS 59*, which moved further north.

In addition to combat with partisans, there were also battles with advancing British troops, specifically the New Zealand 6th Armoured Division. On May 6–7, 1945, the last units reached the crest of the Carnic Alps. I Battalion disbanded there on May 9, 1945, II Battalion about six miles to the east the same day.

While many—especially those from South Tyrol—made their way home, some entire units became prisoners of war of the British. Thus ended the deployment of the *SS Karstjäger*. Envisaged and trained as special mountain troops, the war brought changes in its composition and range of duties.

Expansion of the *SS-Karstwehr-Bataillon* to brigade or division strength could not be realized, not only because of the shortage of officers and NCOs, but also because of shortages of equipment and unavailability of the required personnel. The question remains: why was the unit not brought up to authorized strength using personnel diverted from the large ethnic German contingents from Croatia, Rumania or Hungary or members of the *Luftwaffe* or *Kriegsmarine*, as was common practice in other SS units in 1944–45?

Approximately 100 *SS-Karstjäger* were killed in action during the unit's roughly twenty months of combat duty. If one compares this number to those of formations fighting on the Eastern Front at the same time, it becomes apparent that the SS-*Karstjäger*—despite all the tragedy of the partisan war—were committed in a secondary theater.

Appendix 2: The Anti-Partisan War Badge

Hitler instituted the Anti-Partisan War Badge on January 29, 1944. Regarding this, the press office of the *Wehrmacht* High Command (OKW) released the following:

> The *Führer* instituted the Anti-Partisan War Badge, which will be awarded to German soldiers, or brothers in arms from the allied European states fighting at their side against the partisans organized by Moscow, in the swamps and forests behind the Eastern Front and in the valleys and hills of the mountains of the southeast, as an acknowledgment of their bravery and deeds.

The regulation governing the awarding of the decoration was issued the same day and it formulated the statutes more precisely. Contrary to the press release, the decoration was not limited to any area of operations and not only envisaged for the struggle against Communist partisans:

> I institute the Anti-Partisan War Badge to recognize the efforts in the increasingly well-organized and more fiercely-waged partisan war.
>
> The Anti-Partisan War Badge is a bravery and achievement decoration. The Anti-Partisan War Badge will be awarded in three grades (Bronze, Silver and Gold).
>
> The Anti-Partisan War Badge is to be worn on the left breast side.
>
> Recipients will receive an award document.

The bereaved will retain the Anti-Partisan War Badge in memory of the fallen.

Implementing rules will be issued by the *Reichsführer-SS*.

As the effort against the partisans was primarily a task of the German Police, Hitler left the writing of further award conditions to Himmler, as the commander of police forces. Himmler subsequently released the following on February 1, 1944.

The Anti-Partisan War Badge is a bravery and achievement decoration.

The Anti-Partisan War Badge is to be issued as recognition of achievement in the struggle against the partisans. It will be awarded in three grades (Bronze, Silver, Gold).

The Anti-Partisan War Badge can be awarded to officers, non-commissioned officers and enlisted men of all German units engaged in the war against the partisans.

The conditions for awarding the decoration are:

a) for the first grade (Bronze) = 20 combat days
b) for the second grade (Silver) = 50 combat days
c) for the third grade (Gold) = 100 combat days
5. To be credited as combat days are:

a) for the members of all units seeing action in the infantry role:

Each day in which the members of the unit have the opportunity to make close combat contact with the enemy (man against man). This can thus occur in attack, defense, during patrols, while serving as a runner, repulsing an enemy patrol, etc.

b) for the members of heavy weapon units:

Each day in which the members of these units (gun crews, etc.) see direct action (close combat) with partisans.

For members of flak units engaged in the war against the partisans, in addition to combat days in which the gun crews come into direct action against partisans, those in which the gun crews shoot down an enemy aircraft are also counted.

c) for the crews of individual aircraft or aviation units involved in the war against the partisans:

Each day in which the aircraft crews successfully complete a mission under enemy fire. Each confirmed shooting down of an enemy aircraft counts as three combat days.

The following number of combat days is required as a condition for awarding of the Anti-Partisan War Badge to aircraft crews:

for the first stage (Bronze) = 30 combat days
for the second stage (Silver) = 75 combat days
for the third stage (Gold) = 150 combat days.

Combat days could be assessed retroactively to January 1, 1943, whereby days already counted in the awarding of the Close Combat Clasp may not be counted again for the Anti-Partisan War Badge. Fifteen close combat days are required for the awarding of the 1st Grade of the Close Combat Clasp, therefore a maximum of just fourteen days can be used retroactively.

On August 4, 1944, the Army High Command (OKH) directed that henceforth the Close Combat Clasp could only be awarded for combat against regular troops. Close combat against partisans thus remained the exclusive basis for the awarding of the Anti-Partisan War Badge. Until that time, close combat against partisans could also be recognized for awarding the Close Combat Clasp.

This was also the reason for the institution of the new decoration. After the assumption was obviously made that close combat against—mainly untrained—partisans/civilians could not be compared to that against regular troops, more close combat days had to be proved in comparison to comparable grades of the Close Combat Clasp:

Variants of the Anti-Partisan War Badge

Semi-hollow back version with a blunt, thin pin and two openings in the area of the hydra.

Semi-hollow back version with a broad, bulbous pin and two openings in the area of the hydra.

Solid version with a broad, bulbous pin and three openings in the area of the hydra.

Semi-hollow back version with a pointed, thin pin and three openings in the area of the hydra.

Anti-Partisan War Badge in Gold

Heinrich Himmler reserved awarding the Anti-Partisan War Badge in Gold to himself and had special solid badges made for this purpose. They had a slightly bulbous pin, three openings, and a blued blade on the front.

Appendix 2: The Anti-Partisan War Badge

The Anti-Partisan War Badge in Gold with Diamonds

Only about twenty examples of the Anti-Partisan War Badge in Gold with Diamonds were made by the C.E. Juncker company in Berlin. Made of silver, the badge had twenty-six small diamonds on the sun wheel and was probably envisaged for honorary awards.

	Close Combat Clasp	Anti-Partisan Badge
1st Grade (Bronze)	15 close combat days	20 close combat days
2nd Grade (Silver)	30 close combat days	50 close combat days
3rd Grade (Gold)	50 close combat days	100 close combat days

Combat days to be counted were calculated based on recommendations by company commanders were to be issued by the commanding officers of independent battalions, regiments, etc., in orders of the day. Initially each man was supposed to carry an insert in his paybook, on which these operational days were confirmed by the company commander. These were later done away with to prevent soldiers from suffering disadvantage in the event of capture.

In fact there was frequent misinterpretation in determining a partisan combat day. As a rule, days were counted in which the man had been in simple combat <u>without</u> experiencing close combat against partisans. In regard to this, several members of the *SS-Karstwehr-Bataillon* decorated with the Anti-Partisan War Badge stated that they had never engaged in close combat with partisans.

When, on August 25, 1944, Himmler requested reports on men who were supposed to be awarded the Anti-Partisan War Badge in Gold, this misinterpretation became quite obvious. The following letter was subsequently sent to the positions submitting the recommendations:

> The *Reichsführer-SS* has once again emphatically pointed out that the strictest measures must be use in determining partisan combat days and that only actual close combat days are to be considered for the awarding of the Anti-Partisan War Badge.

As previously mentioned, it turned out that the award conditions had for the most part been wrongly interpreted. On October 12, 1944, *SS-Sturmbannführer* Kment, adjutant to the *Reichsführer-SS*, wrote the following to *SS-Obergruppenführer und General der Waffen-SS* Wolff, the Supreme SS and Police Commander in Italy:

> Before I can submit your applications for the awarding and presentation of the Anti-Partisan War Badge in Gold, the recommendations must first be closely scrutinized by the command headquarters there. The recommendations submitted by you on September 27, 1944, which I have returned in the appendix, do not create the impression that those recommended have been in combat man against man one hundred times in the specified periods of time.

As the initial focus was limited to submissions for the awarding of the Anti-Partisan War Badge in Gold, it is reasonable to conclude that a considerable number of the Anti-Partisan War Badges in Bronze and Silver were awarded contrary to the regulations. According to various former SS-*Karstjäger*, this is also shown in the awarding of the decoration to various senior officers and commanders. For example, it is safe to assume that *SS-Standartenführer* Dr. Brand, the sixty-five-year-old commander of the *SS-Karstwehr-Bataillon*, did not go through 20 or 50 days of close combat with partisans. In addition to his extreme corpulence and a larynx ailment, he had just one eye and papillary rigidity in that one. His receipt of the Anti-Partisan War Badge in Bronze can therefore only be attributed to an acknowledgment of his actions or merely the already-discussed misinterpretation of the expression "partisan combat day." *SS-Gruppenführer* Globocnik, the Senior SS and Police Commander in the Adriatic Coastland zone of operations, wrote the following to Dr. Brand in a letter dated February 23, 1945:

> Concerning your Anti-Partisan War Badge, I am happy to be able to inform you that it is already on its way to you, and I hope that it has arrived before this letter. Please accept my

> congratulations for the decoration. Because of new orders, the *Waffen-Gebirgs-Karstjäger-Brigade* is in no longer attached to me in any way, and I therefore had only limited influence in the awarding of the Anti-Partisan War Badge to you.
>
> In procuring the information necessary for the awarding of the Anti-Partisan War Badge I am bound by the very strict guidelines of the *Reichsführer-SS*. I am sorry that the KJB could not provide any other information. I can therefore not make any change, but I hope that you will be happy with the Bronze.

On March 9, 1945, it was again pointed out that only "*close combat days*" were acceptable. The writings of *SS-Sturmbannführer* Wenner, adjutant to the Supreme SS and Police Commander in Italy, document this:

> With respect to this, I would particularly like to stress that in many cases applications are being submitted based on information taken from soldiers' paybooks. Practice has shown, however, that in many cases the point was misunderstood when it came to entries of partisan combat days, in that not only close combat days, but also the slightest enemy contact, even including regular service days, were logged.

Corresponding to different units, different commands were authorized to award the decoration, and Himmler reserved to himself—not least for the named reasons—the right to award the 3rd Grade:

> a) The *Reichsführer-SS*
> b) The Commander of Anti-Partisan Units for members of the staffs of the Senior SS and Police Commander and all units of the police, *Waffen-SS* and *Wehrmacht* directly attached to him.

SS-Sturmbannführer Kühbandner was one of the few wearers of the Anti-Partisan War Badge in Gold.

c) The Senior SS and Police Commander for the units of the *Waffen-SS*, the police and the *Wehrmacht* directly attached to him.
d) Tactical superiors with the powers of at least a division commander for all army soldiers attached to him.
e) The Commander-in-Chief of a Naval Group or Naval High Command for members of the navy.
f) The commanding general for members of the *Luftwaffe*.

The badge could also be awarded to someone who had almost fulfilled the necessary conditions, if the recipient, because of wounds, was no longer in a position to completely reach the required number of partisan combat days. Awarding the decoration under these circumstances was also reserved for the *Reichsführer-SS*.

The decoration could be awarded to any German soldier and foreign volunteers who had sworn an oath to Hitler. From October 5, 1944, the eligibility criteria were expanded to include, "persons who are not members of the *Wehrmacht*, the *Waffen-SS* or the police but have actively participated in the combating of partisans." Thus, for example, in addition to members of the state railway (*Reichsbahn*), theoretically forest workers in the occupied areas who were attacked by partisans in the many forests could also be decorated.

In total, six members of the *24. Waffen-Gebirgs[Karstjäger]-Division der SS* were decorated with the Anti-Partisan War Badge in Gold on February 15, 1945, and March 10, 1945. In fact, it might reasonably be assumed that even these ten soldiers had not experienced 100 days of close combat. In the case of *SS-Obersturmführer* Prasch, for example, the award application reveals that the information concerning partisan combat days was based on "his information."

As the different number of close combat days for the three grades of the Anti-Partisan War Badge compared to those for the Close Combat Clasp show, so called "anti-partisan warfare" was basically valued less than action against regular troops. So there was no "automatic" awarding of the Iron Cross, First Class or the German Cross in Gold to recipients of the Anti-Partisan War Badge in Silver or Gold. While Hitler laid down that holders of the Close Combat Clasp in Gold could be awarded the German Cross in Gold without any further justification, as fifty days of close combat demonstrably brought with them very special bravery and daring, seven of the ten wearers of the Anti-Partisan War Badge in Gold did not even have the Iron Cross, Second Class or the Wound Badge in Black (sic!) before they were decorated. Surely this is further proof that the 100 partisan combat days had not been close combat days.

The badge, which was worn on the left breast side, was 1.89 by 2.28 inches in size and had an oak leave wreath, in the center of which was a Germanic sword thrust into a five-headed hydra. In Greek mythology the hydra was a nine-headed snake-like creature, which grew two new heads for each one cut off. Beneath the sword handle is a sun wheel and beneath the hydra a death's head.

There were different manufacturing variants, which differed as follows:

> A solid (full) version with a broad, bulbous pin. The outstanding feature was the three holes in the area of the hydra.
>
> A solid (full) version with a thin, round pin. This version had no holes in the area of the hydra.
>
> A semi-hollow back version with a broad, bulbous pin. This appeared with two or three or no holes in the area of the hydra.
>
> A semi-hollow back version with a blunt, thin, round pin. There were two holes in the area of the hydra.
>
> A semi-hollow back version with a pointed, thin, round pin. This badge was produced with three holes in the area of the hydra.

A solid (full) version of the 3rd Grade of non-ferrous metal, which had the distinguishing feature of a burnished blade of the Germanic sword. This decoration was made for presentation by Himmler.

A solid (full) version of the 3rd Grade in silver with twenty-six small diamonds on the sun wheel. These twenty Anti-Partisan War Badges were probably envisaged, like the joint Pilot and Observer Badges with Diamonds, for honorary awards.

With the exception of the last two variants, as a rule Anti-Partisan War Badges were made of high-grade zinc and alloyed in keeping with the grade.

The number of Anti-Partisan War Badges awarded can only be estimated. As within about half a year after the decoration was instituted there were almost no remaining partisan combat zones apart from the *Generalgouvernement* (Poland) and southeastern Europe, the potential number of decorations awarded is rather small. Of the more than 500,000 soldiers and police members involved in guarding the rear areas, probably about 3,000 were awarded the badge in bronze, approximately 800 in silver, and ten in gold.*

By comparison: of the more than ten-million members of the army, only about 650 soldiers received the Close Combat Clasp in Gold. The number of required close combat days was fifty, precisely the number needed for the Anti-Partisan War Badge in Silver.

*Also of interest in this regard is *SS-Sonderkommando "Dirlewanger,"* which was constantly in action against partisans from spring 1942 to autumn 1944. After the institution of the Anti-Partisan War Badge, in February 1944, the unit requested twenty badges in gold, thirty in silver, and 200 in bronze. In fact, not a single Grade 3 decoration was awarded by the end of the war and the Anti-Partisan War Badge in Bronze and Silver in only a few cases.